MALAYSIA

Heidi Munan

MARSHALL CAVENDISH
New York • London • Sydney

Reference edition published 1993 by
Marshall Cavendish Corporation
2415 Jerusalem Avenue
P.O. Box 587
North Bellmore
New York 11710

Originated and designed by
Times Books International, an imprint of
Times Editions Pte Ltd

Printed in Singapore

Library of Congress Cataloging-in-Publication Data:
Munan, Heidi, 1941–
    Malaysia / Heidi Munan.
        p. cm.—(Cultures Of The World)
    Includes bibliographical references.
    Summary: Introduces the geography, history,
    religious beliefs, government, and people of
    Malaysia.
    ISBN 1-85435-296-2
    1. Malaysia—Juvenile literature. [1. Malaysia.]
I. Title. II. Series.
DS592.M85 1990
959.5—dc20   89–25464
                    CIP
                    AC

Cultures of the World

Editorial Director	Shirley Hew
Managing Editors	Mark Dartford
	Shova Loh
Editors	Goh Sui Noi
	Meena Mylvaganam
	Cheryl M. English
Picture Editor	Jane Duff
Production	Edmund Lam
	Robert Paulley
	Julie Cairns
Design	Tuck Loong
	Doris Nga
	Stella Liu
	Lee Woon Hong
Illustrators	Francis Oak
	Thomas Koh
	Vincent Chew

INTRODUCTION

 Malaysia is a land of diversity. It is a land of diverse races, diverse cultures, diverse languages, diverse religions. Yet Malaysia is one of the most stable nations in the region, an emerging industrial power to be reckoned with. It is a leader in the affairs of ASEAN (Association of Southeast Asian Nations) and a respected voice in world affairs.

This does not mean that Malaysia is a thoroughly urbanized and modernized nation. Beside the motorways lie rural villages of palm-thatched houses. A multi-story office block is inaugurated by the chanting of Buddhist priests or the solemn reading of a Moslem blessing. Jet aircraft soar over flooded paddy fields plowed by patient buffaloes.

This book, part of the series Cultures of the World, will help you understand the riddles and reconcile the seeming contradictions that is Malaysia. The land is not inaccessible, the people are not inscrutable.

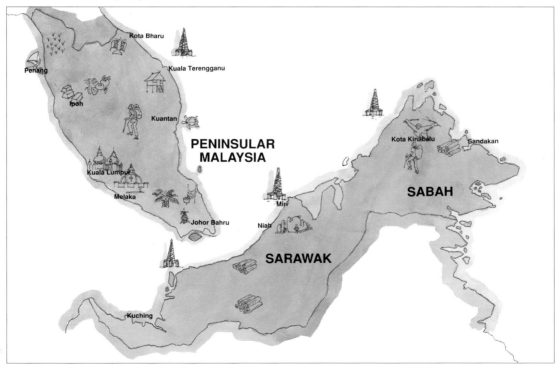

CONTENTS

Getting used to his holiday costume. Malay children are dressed in traditional costumes on special occasions, especially Malay festivals.

CONTENTS

An Iban in his splendid headdress. Ibans are one of the main tribes in East Malaysia.

GEOGRAPHY

GEOGRAPHICAL LOCATION

MALAYSIA consists of two parts, East, and West or Peninsular Malaysia, an area of 127,581 square miles separated by about 330 miles of the South China Sea.

Peninsular Malaysia is the Malay Peninsula, the Golden Chersonese mentioned by writers of antiquity. East Malaysia is situated on the northern fringe of the world's third largest island, Borneo. Both parts of Malaysia lie in the equatorial rainfall zone, immediately north of the equator but below the hurricane belt. In the days of sailing ships, the harbors in the Melaka Straits and on the southern tip of the Peninsula were often used by traders to weather the monsoons which raged in the South China Sea.

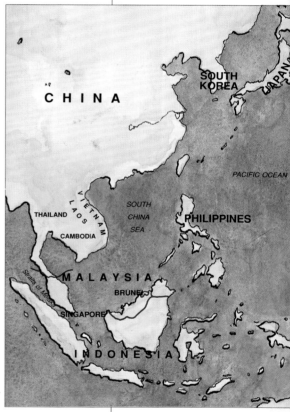

SEASONS

Malaysia has two seasons—wet and very wet. Rain falls daily during the monsoon season from October to April, but even during the supposedly "dry" period there are a couple of showers per week. Kuala Lumpur recorded 185 rainy days in 1986, Kota Kinabalu 167; Kuching holds the record of 248!

Air humidity is high all the year round, from 60% to 73% at two o'clock in the afternoon.

Temperatures in Malaysia range from 77°F to 95°F, with mostly cool nights. "Cool" means that in hilly areas it is advisable to use a light blanket as cover; in the low-lying parts a cotton sheet is enough.

Above: **Malaysia and her neighbors.**

Left: **Warm sunshine, white sandy beach and waving palms. Malaysia is all these and more.**

PENINSULAR MALAYSIA

The eleven States of Peninsular Malaysia extend from Johor Darul Takzim in the south to the Thai border in the north, including a few offshore islands.

The Peninsula's backbone of mountains, Banjaran Titiwangsa, runs north to south with short rivers draining into either the Melaka Straits to the west, or the South China Sea to the east. The mountain range rises to over 6,500 feet in places and is a serious obstacle to east-west traffic. A road from Kuala Lumpur to Kuantan was completed in 1911, another to Kota Bharu after 1980.

All Malaysian States have access to the sea, from tiny Perlis Indra Kayangan (307 sq miles), tucked away between Kedah Darul Aman and Thailand, to majestic Pahang Darul Makmur (13,886 sq miles) in the Peninsula's center. Kedah is a land of fertile plains devoted to rice-growing while huge estates of oil palm, cocoa and rubber now utilize the lowlands of Johor.

Kelantan Darul Naim and Terengganu Darul Iman are east of the main mountain range. Undulating plains lie open to the South China Sea which traditionally yields a living to the fearless fishermen living in these States.

Perak Darul Ridzwan, Selangor Darul Ehsan and Negeri Sembilan Darul Khusus occupy the west coast south of Kedah. Tin ore is found in these three States, giving them corresponding political and economic importance in the 19th century.

Melaka was an important trading port until the Portuguese came in 1511. Penang Island or Pulau Pinang rose to prominence in the late 18th century.

Above: **Kedah is a land of fertile plains devoted to rice-growing.**

Opposite: **Map of Peninsular Malaysia.**

EAST MALAYSIA

East Malaysia lies on Borneo, north of the Indonesian province of Kalimantan. The two East Malaysian States, Sarawak and Sabah, share many physical characteristics. For both states, rivers formed the most common transport routes until quite recent times, and the main settlements were within the tidal estuaries. Jungle produce, birds' nests and other rarities were early exports.

Sabah occupies 28,425 square miles of Borneo's northeastern corner. Its profile is dominated by the Crocker Range whose highest peak is Mt. Kinabalu. The chain of mountains continues southward forming the watershed between Sarawak and Kalimantan. Sabah's main rivers drain into the Sulu Sea, where Sandakan, the territory's first center, is situated. The capital, Kota Kinabalu, lies on the west coast.

Of Sarawak's 47,871 square miles, only about one-fifth is really suitable for agriculture. Wide tracts of the coast are covered in mangrove swamps or semi-saline swamp forest, sources of many natural products but otherwise agriculturally unproductive. Sarawak's capital, Kuching, lies in the State's western corner.

Sarawak's main rivers, the Rajang and the Baram, rise in the highlands along the State's eastern fringe.

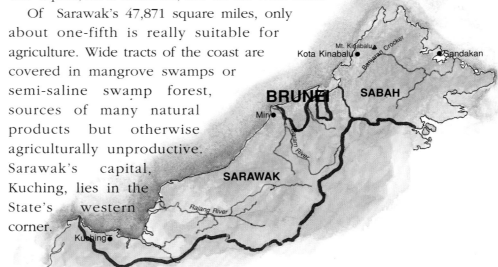

Kuala Lumpur, or Muddy Estuary, is today a major modern capital, with sleek glass-and-steel skyscrapers (left) and six-lane motorways chock-a-block with spanking new cars including Mercedes Benz, BMWs and Volvos—a far cry from the early days of independence (below).

KUALA LUMPUR

Kuala Lumpur is Malaysia's capital, a town grown from a Chinese tin mining settlement in the Sultan of Selangor's territory. The original township stood on the confluence of the Gombak and Klang rivers, which explains its name: Kuala means "confluence" or "estuary;" Lumpur means "muddy."

Drainage is still something of a problem. Flash floods bring traffic in low-lying areas to a standstill during the heavy monsoon rains.

Kuala Lumpur is called the Federal Territory and is administered separately from its "parent State," Selangor. Centrally located on the west coast of the Malay Peninsula, it is the seat of the Malaysian Government. The National University, National Mosque, and the head offices of most big business concerns are also located here.

Like many Southeast Asian cities, Kuala Lumpur attracts a daily inflow of migrants from the rural areas who live in congested urban *kampung* or quickly constructed squatter villages.

By the way, only the newsreader on the radio refers to the nation's capital as "Kuala Lumpur." It is popularly known as "K.L."

The sandy beaches of Batu Ferringhi along the northern shore of Penang attract sun-seekers all the year round.

PENANG

Penang Island or Pulau Pinang, founded by British East India Company Captain Francis Light in the 18th century, was an important trading station in the Malay Peninsula during the 19th century. However, it declined in importance when Singapore, off the southern tip of the Peninsula, rose to prominence in the 1820s.

Penang had a good natural harbor where ship captains could wait out the fierce monsoon, do a little quiet trading in Kedah, Perlis, Perak or Sumatra, and then return to Calcutta in India after the winds had changed.

Penang still relies on commerce for a living, including the tourist trade. Tin from southern Thailand and Perak is smelted in Penang. Rubber-processing, textile manufacture and food production are sited here. Thai rice is imported in bulk and redistributed throughout Malaysia from Penang.

Ferries regularly ply between George Town on the island, and Butterworth on the mainland. Regular air services also link Penang to the Peninsula and the world.

Since 1985, the world's third-longest bridge ties Penang firmly to Province Wellesley on the mainland. The 8.4-mile bridge was built at a cost of US$295 million, and opened by the Prime Minister, who personally drove a Malaysia-made car, the Proton Saga, across it.

TRANSPORT

Transport in both East and Peninsular Malaysia has traditionally been by water. However, river transport is no longer important in Peninsular Malaysia except on parts of the east coast. In East Malaysia, river transport remains a major means of communication with many settlements accessible only by water.

Peninsular Malaysia has one of Southeast Asia's best road networks. There are three major highways: one runs from the Malaysian/Thai border in the north along the west coast to the southern tip of the Peninsula; the second links Port Kelang on the west coast to Kuantan on the east coast; and Route III runs along the

east coast from Kuantan northward to Kota Bharu. The road network in East Malaysia is inferior to that in the Peninsula. Rail transport is also well developed in Peninsular Malaysia. There is no railway system in Sarawak, while the old Sabah Railway between Kota Kinabalu and Tenom has been partially opened.

Coastal and sea transport systems in Malaysia are important, given the long coastlines. Coastal and river ports include George Town and Port Kelang in Peninsular Malaysia, and Kuching, Sibu, Labuan, Kota Kinabalu, Sandakan and Tawau in East Malaysia.

Air transport is growing rapidly and is an important link between East and Peninsular Malaysia, with regular internal services between Kuala Lumpur, Kuching, and Kota Kinabalu. Also, a fleet of small aircraft maintains vital links in the remote areas of East Malaysia.

The Malaysian railway system is largely confined to the Peninsula, with a total of 994 miles of tracks serving 38 domestic stations. In the south, the railway line extends into Singapore, while in the north, a line connects with the State Railway of Thailand, thus enabling travel by rail to the two neighboring countries.

WILDLIFE

Malaysia's best-known National Park is Taman Negara in Pahang. Set in 1,677 square miles of dense tropical forest surrounding the East Coast Range, it includes Gunung Tahan (7,121 feet), the highest peak in Peninsular Malaysia.

Taman Negara is linked to the outside world only by river. Kuala Tembeling is the last contact point for road and rail travelers. From there the journey to Kuala Tahan and chalet-style lodgings at the foot of the mountain continues by boat.

The flora and fauna of Southeast Asia are painstakingly preserved in Taman Negara, making this a paradise for bird-watchers, butterfly hunters (only with a camera), simian fanciers, or the stout of heart who do not mind an encounter with a tiger or a wild buffalo—both rare but extant in this National Park.

In Sarawak, there are Bako National Park, protecting a slice of coastal and lowland forest for posterity, and Niah National Park with its spectacular limestone caves. No National Park is easy of access, and Niah is no exception: a bumpy 112-mile drive from Miri takes the visitor to Batu Niah; from there, a short boat ride will land him at Pengkalan Lobang; a two-and-a-half mile walk through the park's 7,668 acres, partly on a plank walk, will finally bring him to the caves' West Mouth.

In Taman Negara, hides like the one below make it possible to observe jungle animals in safety. At 16 feet above ground, they are out of the reach of elephants.

MOUNT KINABALU

At 13,328 feet, Mt. Kinabalu is the highest peak in Southeast Asia. Rising within view of the sea, it actually seems to be "near as high as Mt. Everest" as a startled World War II pilot exclaimed when the huge mass rose in front of his fragile craft.

Mt. Kinabalu is the center of one of Malaysia's most popular National Parks, 291 square miles of lowland rain forest, hill forest, "cloud forest" as mossy vegetation shrouded in mist and moisture is called, sub-alpine grass patches, and the summit area of bare, wind-scrubbed granite.

Mt. Kinabalu is a botanist's dream. The parasitical rafflesia with its three-foot bloom is found here, as are fungi, including the "sunburst," and fern trees thirteen feet high. Ground orchids, tree orchids, cliff orchids, the tiny podochilus only just visible to the naked eye, are all found wild in this park. The rain forest of Kinabalu Park teems with nepenthes, plants that carry graceful pitchers up to seven pints in content to catch live prey.

Most of Malaysia's wildlife can be met in Kinabalu Park. Bats and squirrels, shrews and tarsiers, and the slow loris which really is quite slow! Monkeys and apes, including the friendly orang utan thrive in this protected area; the scaly anteater is safe from greedy gourmets here, as are many species of deer and wild pigs, and the nearly three hundred species of birds.

Above: **An orang utan at play.**

Below: **The wild, wind-swept summit of Mt. Kinabalu or Akin Nabalu, "home of the spirits of the departed."**

Niah cave paintings and burial boats.

HISTORY

PREHISTORY

HISTORY is not necessarily found in books. Early Man left pot sherds, worked stone and wood fragments, traces of villages and towns and scraped a record of his doings into the walls of primitive rock shelters.

The Malaysian climate is no preserver of such remains: hewn wood rots within a few decades; metals deteriorate; stone structures are soon invaded and obliterated by the jungle. Malaysia's prehistory is pieced together from finds in caves, burial sites, ritual deposits interred in dry, gravelly soils. It is none the less fascinating.

Humans were living in Niah Caves in Sarawak 35,000 years ago, as an adolescent's skull found there has proved. Red-earth paintings on the cave walls show men paddling boats, hunting mysterious animals and a scene that could be a dance. From a later date there are boat-shaped coffins in which the dead were thought to float down the big river into the next world. Little is known about who the early Niah people were, but they had developed crafts such as pot-making and simple weaving.

Pottery and stone implements were found in Gua Cha, a cave in Kelantan. Fragments of rough boats hauled up into dry shelters show that the early settlers built usable craft with stone tools.

Every now and then, an adze or a chopper is found somewhere. Colorful pebbles laboriously drilled indicate that some man, thousands of years ago, made beads for a purpose we can but guess at—to give himself magical strength, to fasten his simple garments, or to present to the lady of his heart?

Remains found in Gua Cha, Kedah, indicate that, after 2000 B.C., Neolithic immigrants from southwestern China brought with them an advanced material culture including pottery of high aesthetic and functional quality.

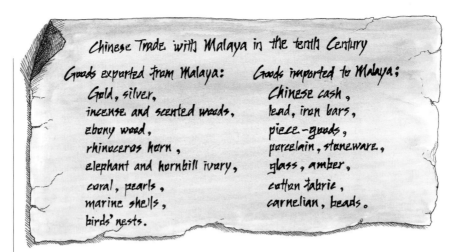

Chinese Trade with Malaya in the tenth Century

Goods exported from Malaya:	Goods imported to Malaya:
Gold, silver,	Chinese cash,
incense and scented woods,	lead, iron bars,
ebony wood,	piece-goods,
rhinoceros horn,	porcelain, stoneware,
elephant and hornbill ivory,	glass, amber,
coral, pearls,	cotton fabric,
marine shells,	carnelian, beads.
birds' nests.	

Chinese traders joined the early settlements, to exchange Indian for Chinese goods and to buy up the Peninsula's produce. It is from Chinese historians that we know what goods were in demand, at what sort of prices, and how the period's "barbarians" of the Malay Peninsula dressed and behaved.

EARLY ASIAN CONTACTS

The Malay Peninsula is situated halfway between India and China. Its position makes it the natural entrepot between these two giants. It is surmised that early traders met and bartered goods in sheltered places along the Melaka Straits and the Peninsula's southern tip centuries before any one boat was prepared to undertake the whole long, dangerous journey from Calcutta to Shanghai.

These foreign traders and settlers, and others who came centuries later, brought their religions and their ways of life with them, but they did not settle in significant numbers. Hinduism and Buddhism have left cultural traces, artefacts as well as customs which were absorbed into local folk-ways. Many Malay wedding customs may be traced back to a dim Hindu past.

MELAKA

The foundation of the first powerful state on the Melaka Straits is shrouded in legend. A princeling called Parameswara, exiled from his native Sumatra, founded a pirate base on Temasek (Singapore). Being a less than popular ruler, he was later expelled and fled to the fishing village of Melaka where he made himself master.

Geography and the trade patterns of the day assisted Parameswara's undoubted abilities: Melaka grew into a trading center important enough to attract the jealousy of the Siamese, and the protection of China, the distant overlord of most of Southeast Asia then.

What is left of the Fort built by the Portuguese in 1511.

18

Numerous Indian traders settled in Melaka. They brought Islam to the Straits in the early 15th century. The history of Melaka under its Indianized Malay court is a tale of intrigue and heroism.

Melaka's last chief minister, Tun Mutahir, made the fatal mistake of trying to fool the Portuguese when they sailed into the Straits in 1509. He launched a sneak attack on the foreign vessels in port. Most of the intruders escaped, only to return with reinforcements, to take revenge on the treacherous "Moors," as they called all Moslems.

George Town, Penang, in the 1890s. Penang gave the British a foothold on the vital India-China route, which increased in importance as China tea became a fashionable drink in Europe.

The tall "tea clippers" were marvels of speed and elegance under sail. Prizes were given to the captain and crew of the first ship to bring the year's fresh harvest to England.

WESTERN CONTACTS

The Portuguese were the first western nation to raise their flag in the Straits. They took Melaka in 1511 and built a fort, a church and a customs house.

They did not live happily ever after. The exiled Sultan had established himself in Johor on the southern tip of the Peninsula. From there, he tried to regain his dominion. Other powerful Malay States in the region resented the Christian intruders' attempts at creating a trade monopoly. Sea rovers and pirates were encouraged to attack foreign shipping. Legitimate trade declined as bigger, better equipped vessels chose to sail west of Sumatra on their way to Batavia, rather than risk running the pirate gauntlet of the Melaka Straits.

The Dutch who had established themselves in West Java in the early 17th century took Melaka in 1641, after which the town's importance declined rapidly. The island of Penang, acquired by the British in 1786, became the only important foreign trading base in the Straits.

BRITISH PERIOD

The foundation of Singapore in 1819 and the Anglo-Dutch Treaty of 1824 gave Britain control of the Melaka Straits. *Pax Britannica* attracted migrants: labor was imported from India and China to work tin mines and rubber plantations.

In the 1870s, local conflicts on the Malay Peninsula gave the British an excuse to intervene there. "Advisors" were attached to the Sultans' courts, British officials who practically ruled the States except on matters of religion and local customs.

In 1905, Perak, Pahang, Selangor and Negeri Sembilan were persuaded by the British to unite as the Federated Malay States for administrative convenience.

By this time, the Indian and Chinese communities were making their presence felt. In the 1920s, Malay nationalism stirred while anti-British Chinese political parties were founded. Each community was suspicious of the other, but relied on the British to keep order.

Administratively, Malaya, as the Peninsula was then known, was a hodgepodge: Federated Malay States and Unfederated Malay States under British protection, and the Straits Settlements of Penang, Melaka and Singapore which were in effect British colonies.

When the Japanese army overran Malaya in 1942, just under half the population was Malay; the Chinese made up a third and the Indians about 14%.

THE INGREDIENTS OF MALAYSIA

Malaya obtained its first constitution in 1955 in preparation for independence in 1957. Three main political parties emerged: UMNO (Malay), MCA (Chinese) and MIC (Indian). The first elected Prime Minister was a member of Kedah aristocracy, Tunku Abdul Rahman.

In the early 1960s a new, larger Federation was mooted: Malaysia, which was to include Malaya and Singapore, and Brunei, Sarawak and Sabah on Borneo Island.

Brunei, Sarawak and Sabah had become British colonies after World War II. Before the war, Sarawak had been ruled by the family of James Brooke, while Sabah had been ruled by a chartered company founded by British and foreign trade interests.

In the end, Brunei chose not to join the Federation. Having ascertained the wishes of the peoples of Sarawak and Sabah to its satisfaction, the British Government granted them both independence through joining the Federation of Malaysia, which was declared in 1963.

Singapore left Malaysia in 1965 to become a Republic.

The opening of Parliament by the King. Parliamentary procedure in Malaysia is based on the procedure of the British Parliament, as well as those of the other Commonwealth countries. Since 1967, Malay has been the official language of Parliament although a member may speak in English with the permission of the speaker. Parliament makes decisions by a simple majority, but a two-thirds majority is required in some cases, including certain amendments to the constitution.

GOVERNMENT

MALAYSIA IS A FEDERATION

MALAYSIA is a Federation. Each of its thirteen member States has its own legislature, and may determine certain issues for itself—agricultural and land policy, for instance, differ from State to State.

Furthermore, East Malaysian States have their own immigration laws. A foreigner traveling from Peninsular to East Malaysia needs a passport!

The Federal Parliament consists of two chambers, the House of Representatives and the Senate. Representatives are elected by the people while Senators are appointed by the Yang di-Pertuan Agong (King) or elected by the State legislatures.

Parliament is the legislative arm of government. Its members introduce, debate and approve new laws or amend old ones. One hundred and seventy-seven members meet three or four times a year.

The party which commands a majority in Parliament chooses the Prime Minister, though he is officially appointed by the Yang di-Pertuan Agong. The Prime Minister chooses some of his party's members in the House of Representatives or Senate to be Ministers in charge of various portfolios. This Cabinet is responsible to Parliament and ultimately to the electorate.

In the U.S., one person—the President—fulfills both executive and ceremonial functions. In Malaysia, the two roles are separated: the Prime Minister is the chief executive of the nation, the Yang di-Pertuan Agong the ceremonial Head of State.

The installation of Sultan Azlan Shah of Perak as the Yang di-Pertuan Agong in 1989. Malaysia is a constitutional monarchy with an elected King at its head, the Yang di-Pertuan Agong. This high office is rotated among the nine royal houses of Peninsular Malaysia. At a Rulers' Conference, the nine possible candidates vote for one of their own number to be Head of State for five years. Melaka, Penang, Sabah and Sarawak have no hereditary rulers. In these States the Yang di-Pertuan Agong is represented by a Governor who is not eligible to be elected King.

LOCAL ADMINISTRATION

The smallest administrative unit is the village or longhouse, presided over by a Ketua Kampung (village elder) or Tuai Rumah (house elder). This is usually a political appointment, though in the past elders were elected by the population under their jurisdiction.

A Ketua Kampung is in charge of the smooth functioning of his community: sanitation projects and other community activities are directed by him. He has limited judiciary powers to settle family disputes and infringements of traditional law. In most States he can impose small fines.

In Chinese-populated areas, a Kapitan China (Chinese elder) is appointed with similar limited functions. The rationale for these elders is that a person versed in traditional law and customs should deal with small, everyday matters. In some ways their functions resemble those of a Justice of the Peace.

Most everyday legal matters—issuing of birth, marriage and death certificates and the like—are handled at the District Offices.

The larger towns of Malaysia have Town Boards, Municipal Councils or City Councils. These bodies administer planning, sanitation and building bylaws, issue various licenses and permits, and collect rates for services including refuse collection and road maintenance.

City and Municipal Councils may be appointed or elected, differing from State to State.

An informal discussion between the village elder and some villagers. A Ketua Kampung is responsible for the smooth functioning of his community.

YAHIA CITIZEN AND THE LAW:

A Malaysian may not hold citizenship/passport of any other nation. If he does so he is liable to lose his Malaysian citizenship by process of law.

A Malaysian father remains the legal guardian of his children even if he has divorced their mother.

Non-Moslem Malaysians under 21 years of age cannot get married against their parents' objections. If these objections are unreasonable, a Court Order may be sought to override them, or the couple can wait until both are 21.

Under the Internal Security Act, a Malaysian may be detained without being charged in court if he is suspected of being a threat to public order or the security of the country.

The death penalty is mandatory for persons convicted of drug trafficking; the criminal is usually executed within a few months of conviction.

The judiciary power of Malaysia is vested in the High Court of Malaya and the High Court of Borneo, and in appropriate lower courts. The courts decide civil and criminal cases, or settle the legality of any law or act of government should it be questioned. To enable it to perform its work impartially, the judiciary is independent of political or any other interference.

ECONOMY

MAIN OCCUPATIONS

ROUGHLY TWO-THIRDS of Malaysia's population is classified as "rural," living outside towns. Out of a work force of six million people, two million are engaged in agriculture, fishing and forestry for a living.

In East Malaysia the figures for rural dwellers are proportionately higher, but they are changing for the whole country. By the year 2000, it is estimated that the rural-urban balance will be 50/50. During the 21st century Malaysia will become an increasingly urban society.

The biggest employers are the civil service and the manufacturing industries. These include processing of Malaysia's raw materials (timber, rubber, oil), petroleum refining, and car assembly. One important industry is mining, which traditionally produced tin and gold.

Malaya's oldest known name, "Aurea Chersonesus," means Peninsula of Gold. Gold is still mined in both East and Peninsular Malaysia, not omitting the occasional "gold rush" when villagers scrabble on river banks, washing mud and sand in wide, flat basins searching for the precious metal!

Tin, the Klang Valley product that attracted foreign colonizers in the 19th century, still brings in a portion of Malaysia's foreign earnings.

Mining also includes petroleum production. Crude oil and natural gas are found, mostly in offshore fields in the South China Sea. The main oil-producing States are Terengganu in Peninsular Malaysia and Sabah and Sarawak in East Malaysia.

Above: **Tin-mining. Malaysia is the world's leading producer of tin, accounting for 22% of total world production.**

Opposite: **Collecting sun-dried fish. With such long coastlines, it is no wonder that fishing and related activities are important traditional occupations in Malaysia.**

MALAYSIAN INDUSTRIES

Many Malaysian industries process local raw materials. Timber is made into furniture, veneer and plywood rather than exported as logs. No rubber sandals are imported because home production is more than adequate.

Petroleum products such as chemicals and plastics are made in Malaysia, and some crude oil is refined there as well. The natural gas mined in several large offshore fields in the South China Sea is locally liquefied and exported in that form.

Heavy industry is growing too. In 1987, Malaysia produced 634,050 tons of iron and steel. Nine thousand passenger cars were assembled here, including the Proton Saga, the "national car." Trucks, tractors and other heavy vehicles are also manufactured. In the same year, 31,000 were produced, much in demand in the rural areas where roads are not very good.

Malaysia has a major food industry mainly for the home market. In 1988, it employed nearly 118,000 persons and produced US$293 million worth of sales.

The textile industry kept 78,054 persons busy, many of them girls and women, and grossed US$999 million.

A Proton Saga assembly line. Launched in 1985, the Proton Saga, Malaysia's own national car, has cornered 73% of the total passenger car market.

The construction industry fluctuates with the economic realities of the day. It declined nearly one-third in 1987 to pick up again slowly in 1988. It employs between 300,000 and 500,000 persons. An appreciable number of Malaysian bricklayers are women!

The service industries—including hotels and restaurants, finance and

insurance, and transport and utilities (gas, water, power)—earned US$6.16 billion in 1987.

Tourism, the "invisible export," took fourth place as a foreign exchange earner in 1987, bringing in US$638 million. Malaysia is becoming better known as a holiday destination and air communications are improving. The number of foreign visitors is expected to increase from the present 3.14 million to 3.8 to 4 million in "Visit Malaysia Year 1990."

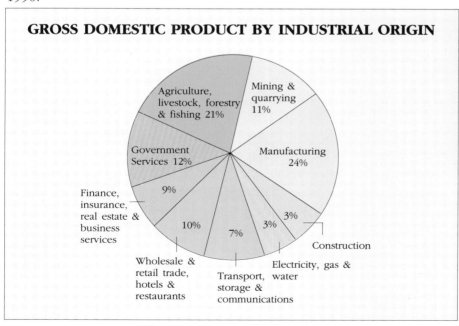

GROSS DOMESTIC PRODUCT BY INDUSTRIAL ORIGIN

Agriculture, livestock, forestry & fishing 21%
Mining & quarrying 11%
Manufacturing 24%
Government Services 12%
Finance, insurance, real estate & business services 9%
Wholesale & retail trade, hotels & restaurants 10%
Transport, storage & communications 7%
Electricity, gas & water 3%
Construction 3%

COTTAGE INDUSTRIES AND RETAIL COMMERCE

In theory, every industry, however small, needs a license in Malaysia. In practice, some "cottage industries" flourish without much supervision.

Many persons from the lower income groups eke out a meager family budget by selling things in the streets, or hawking. Hawkers may retail things such as cigarettes, soft drinks, small goods and secondhand or factory-reject clothing. In many towns there are proper hawkers' centers. However, many hawkers prefer to ply their trade on the footpaths, roadsides, bus stations, parking lots or wherever people congregate. Some hawkers carry their wares in a basket, others spread a mat in any likely spot, ready to vanish if anybody objects to their presence or wants to see a license. More "established" street sellers bring their wares in a trishaw, a three-wheeled bicycle, others have a firmly built or temporary stall to shelter them and their goods from the rain.

Some hawkers have a business license and earn respectable amounts of money. Many of them, however, "fly-by-night" and take to their heels if a policeman is seen coming down the road.

Many Malaysian housewives prepare cakes or snacks for sale, and their small stalls can be seen outside *kampung* houses. During the fasting month of Ramadan whole "night markets" spring up.

Baskets and mats are handmade for sale; now these activities are being co-ordinated under a Handicrafts Development Board. One of Malaysia's most distinctive handicrafts, organized as a small industry in many rural places, is wax-resist fabric dyeing, or *batik*.

Street medicine peddler. Hawkers ply their trade where there is human traffic—footpaths, roadsides, bus stations, even parking lots.

Basket and mat-weaving is a thriving cottage industry, now co-ordinated under a Handicrafts Development Board.

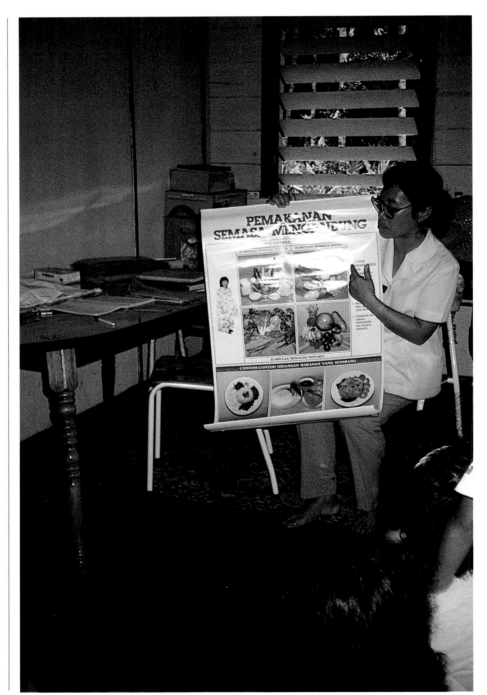

Having done the day's examinations, vaccinations and treatments, Rural Nurse Regina teaches the assembled mothers about nutrition. Regina and her assistant sometimes have to walk many miles on jungle paths to reach her charges, mainly mothers and babies.

A rubber tapper starts the day early, before the sun is up, when many are still snugly in bed. He goes from tree to tree making a V incision, with a sharp knife, on the trunk so that latex flows down into a cup below. After 3 or 4 hours, he makes the rounds again, this time with a bucket to collect the latex which will have filled the cups by now. He finishes work by 10 or 11 in the morning when all the latex is collected and ready to be transported to the factory by trucks.

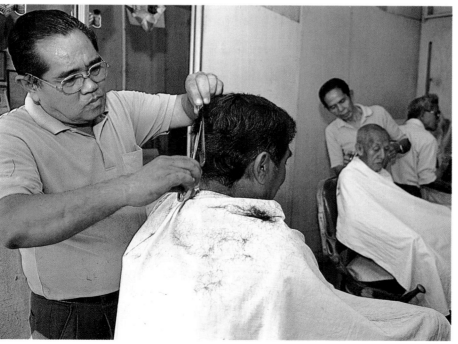

In the city, the little no-frills barbershop-at-the-corner is fast giving way to new "salons" with state-of-the-art hair-dressing paraphernalia.

PEOPLE OF MALAYSIA

HISTORY OF SETTLEMENT

HISTORY and geography have contributed to make Malaysia a truly multiracial country. In jungle areas of both the Malay Peninsula and Borneo, shy aboriginals roam, or learn to settle reluctantly. Over the centuries, they were pressed into the interior by succeeding waves of Proto-Malays who moved in from the northwest.

Within historical times Malays and Chinese arrived. Some stayed on, settling in the fertile river plains.

In 1988, of a total population of 17 million, 59% were Malays and other Bumiputera, or "sons of the soil," 32% were Chinese, 8.2% were Indians.

ORANG ASLI

Interior tribes, called Orang Asli (aboriginal people) in the Peninsula and Penan in Sarawak, are in some cases nomadic jungle folk. At an early age of development, they live by hunting and gathering, staying in rough shelters for a few weeks at a time and then moving on. Many Orang Asli are now learning to grow rice and vegetables, and to rear livestock.

The last generation of true nomads is middle-aged now, and by the end of this century most aboriginals will be settled. Men still go off for the occasional jungle trek, but they come back to a strongly built house they are learning to call home.

Above: **Indian and Chinese stevedores. The turn of the 19th century was a period of large-scale immigration into Malaya. Mines and plantations needed more labor than the country could offer. "Indentured" Chinese and Indian workers were recruited, virtually as slave labor until the cost of the immigrant's fare had been worked off.**

Opposite: **An Orang Asli family at home.**

A traditional Malay house is sturdily built of timber, with a wood-shingled or corrugated iron roof. A front room or verandah provides a cool meeting place for the family; windows cut down to the floor permit air circulation. An industrious man decorates railings, shutters, doors and fascia boards of his home with fretwork.

RURAL MALAY SETTLEMENT

Many Peninsular Malays trace their origin to Sumatra, some having immigrated within the last fifty years. Borneo Malays also have ancestors from that island or from Johor. Malay villages are called *kampung*, settlements of single family houses built by preference in the shelter of a river mouth. Fishing is still a main economic activity of the rural Malays, fish being one of their favorite foods. Every Malay *kampung* has its own mosque or at least a *surau*, a Moslem house of prayer. In the more populated areas of Malaysia, where people of different races live together, the Malay section of a village is often separated from the Chinese bazaar by a small river to make sure no pigs (taboo to Moslems) will invade the *kampung*.

LAND DEVELOPMENT SCHEMES

In rural Malaysia, land development schemes cover thousands of acres with oil palm, rubber, cocoa and other cash crops. Houses for the settlers are usually provided by the developer.

Unlike in a traditional *kampung*, houses on a development scheme are uniform in design, and spread out. Each unit has a small plot of land with it, for growing vegetables or rearing a few chickens. Houses are provided with basic amenities including sanitation, water and electricity and there usually are a school, a rural clinic and a few shops.

EAST MALAYSIAN SETTLEMENTS

The longhouse is the typical dwelling of some East Malaysian natives. It is a row of twelve to fifty or even more houses built side by side, so each shares a wall with its immediate neighbors on either side. The "village street" runs along the front in the form of a wide, covered verandah.

While some people leave the longhouse and move into *kampung*- or urban-style housing, many Borneans still prefer the traditional dwelling. Subsidized public housing in agricultural development areas in Sarawak may be "*kampung*-type" or "longhouse-type," as the settlers wish—and many prefer a modern longhouse of sawn timber, with glass windows and indoor sanitary facilities.

URBAN COMMUNITY

Malaysia is still a predominantly rural country, but the picture is changing rapidly. *Kampung* or longhouse people move into town for a variety of reasons. They hope to find better schools for their children, and better medical and other public facilities. Educated young people look for employment in town.

Urban housing in Malaysia resembles that in other countries. There are roads upon roads full of "terrace houses." Blocks of apartments are becoming common in the larger towns, as are squatter settlements where shacks are constructed out of any materials that come to hand. The climate permits people to live in such flimsy shelters "temporarily," or so they all hope, until they "can afford something better!"

Above left : A longhouse.

Above: The verandah of a longhouse.
Longhouses were built in the past to protect a community. The support pillars could be up to 20 feet high. The notched log that served as a staircase was regularly pulled up at night.

The stone shophouses of Kuala Lumpur's Chinatown. The family business occupies the lower floor, while the upper floor houses the living quarters.

The more conservative Malay women wear over their heads the *telekung mini* (above left), not unlike the nun's wimple, while some Indian women wear updated versions of the traditional tunic and trousers (above right).

THE TAILOR MAKES THE MAN

Malaysians wear summer clothes all the year round. Although urban houses and offices are often air-conditioned, nobody needs sweaters!

For everyday wear, Malaysian men choose a western-style shirt and slacks, or a suit if their position demands it. Women don western dresses, blouses and skirts.

Many Malay women wear modern versions of the *baju kurung*, a gracefully flowing knee-length blouse worn over a floor-length skirt. Indian women are often seen in a gossamer *sari*, their Sikh sisters in a knee-long silk blouse worn over tight trousers of the same material.

While the classical high-necked, high-slit Chinese *cheongsam* is not much in fashion now, the *sam foo* suit of a fitted floral blouse and matching pants is worn by many girls who work in food stalls and similar occupations. It looks smart and is practical.

All Malaysian schoolchildren wear the same uniforms. For primary school students it is white and navy. Secondary schoolgirls wear a white blouse and turquoise pinafore, boys white shirts and army-green pants. Moslem schoolgirls may wear a white *baju kurung* over a blue long skirt. The more pious among them swathe their heads in scarves or white veils worn over tight-fitting caps. They are not allowed to cover their faces—the education authorities want to be quite sure that the person sitting an examination is the candidate herself, and not somebody else!

Moslem women may cover their heads with a veil, though this is not considered necessary for ordinary purposes. It is compulsory only for attending mosque, or saying prayers at home. The very orthodox follow a recently imported fashion of covering their faces in public, known as purdah.

Moslem men cover their heads when engaged in devotions, commonly a rimless black hat called *songkok* which may also be worn for everyday purposes.

Sikh boys of conservative families wear their hair uncut and covered, in a tight topknot wrapped in a silk handkerchief. Their elder brothers and fathers wear the traditional turban, thirty feet of fine muslin wound over a loose-fitting cap. Sikh women should wear a veil when going outdoors, but this restriction is not taken too seriously by the younger set.

Moslems in their holiday best at the mosque during Hari Raya Puasa, a Moslem festival.

Chinese children may be dressed up in traditional robes for Chinese New Year.

HOLIDAY WEAR AND TRADITIONAL COSTUMES

Indian and Malay women often wear their traditional clothes on weekdays and to work. For holidays, all Malaysians make an effort to look smart—appearing at a festival in shabby clothes is considered disrespectful to the host and to the occasion!

Malay boys and girls are dressed up in miniature versions of the adult costume, and usually deport themselves with the utmost gravity at ceremonies.

Chinese children may be dressed up in traditional robes or trouser-suits for the New Year, but this is more common for girls. Few boys above the age of six would care to be seen in "silk pajamas" and a red-buttoned hat by their school friends!

East Malaysians bring out their festive costumes for holiday occasions. Most of these are colorful and picturesque, tradition combined with modern additions like shiny satin, glittering sequins, paper flowers and—the very latest—priceless heirloom silver jewelry imitated in thick tin foil! This substitution is popular for costuming schoolchildren for concerts and the like. If the real antique silver was lost or damaged, the loss could run into thousands of dollars!

A Melanau couple in their festive costume; the tunics are of shiny satin, a modern addition.

LIFESTYLE

ATTITUDES

"A MALAYSIAN runs into a clinic, blood pouring from his head. He inquires after the doctor's and his family's health, not omitting grandma. After a few remarks about the weather he admits he's had a little bother with a brick falling off a building…"

This exaggerated story has a germ of truth in it: Malaysians are a reserved people, given to ceremonious politeness that seems pointless to an outside observer. Rules of behavior must be carefully observed within the family and one's own circle of friends although "people we don't know" are, somehow, outside this framework.

There are personal disagreements between parents and children from time to time, but nobody seriously doubts that the elders' blessing, however formalized, is necessary for "good future, prosperity, health and long life," to quote a common congratulatory formula. Malay boys and girls kiss their parents' hands and beg forgiveness on Hari Raya, the end of Ramadan. Chinese children kneel before their elders on Chinese New Year.

The whole performance seems incredibly embarrassing to foreigners while the parties involved see nothing strange in it. On the other hand, many Malaysians cringe at public hugging and kissing. Now *that* is embarrassing!

"I blush just to see them!" comments an elderly Malay, of western tourists greeting friends at the airport, "in front of everybody, too…"

Above: **On Chinese New Year's day Chinese children pay respects by offering Mandarin oranges to their elders, on their knees.**

Opposite: **Malay boys and girls kiss their parents' hands and beg for forgiveness on Hari Raya, the end of Ramadan.**

STRONG FAMILY TIES

Traditionally, most Malaysians lived within easy reach of their close relatives. Villagers were likely to marry within their own or a neighboring community; any joyous or sad event was shared with a big crowd of cousins, aunts and uncles. However small a house, there is always room for a relative to stay for a few days…or a few weeks…or a few years!

It never fails to astonish Malaysians when foreign friends casually admit that they do not know all their own second cousins. A Malaysian certainly does—and he knows what to call them: elder cousin, younger cousin, eldest aunt, youngest uncle. Names are not much used within the family context; everybody has a "status name." Baby is called "worm" or something similar to protect it from the jealousy of evil spirits.

Traditionally, after marriage, children do not set up home on their own. Rather, an extension to the house is built to accommodate the newlyweds. The extended household is usually big and noisy with grandparents, siblings and their spouses and many grandchildren.

Recent immigrants have kept up their family connections with the "old country," be it China, India, Sumatra or wherever. Some conservative Indian parents make sure their children marry into a suitable family by contacting a matchmaker in the Indian subcontinent to arrange a match for a son or daughter. These arrangements do not always come to fruition: the young people may have different ideas, though they usually feel bad about disobeying their parents on so vital a point.

Most Malaysian societies have ritualized the in-law relationship. Rudeness to in-laws is unpardonable—even a person who does not much like his mother-in-law would consider western jokes on the topic in very bad taste.

BIRTH—RITES AND TABOOS

Malaysian women share a deep concern for their married daughters' and grandchildren's welfare. Pregnant women and newborn babies are guarded against all harm.

The father-to-be has to watch his step too. Among some communities he is not allowed to kill anything, not even a snake, because the unborn baby would be marked if he did!

Two things pregnant or newly delivered mothers of all races are kept away from are "cold" and "wind." "Cold" foods like vegetables and fruit are out; as for iced drinks, forget them! The mother's head is swathed in cloth to keep the "wind" out. Chinese mothers are fed on chicken soup with wine and herbs for forty days to keep them warm, and they cannot shampoo their hair for the duration—never mind how hot and sticky they feel. No newborn baby may be taken outside—"wind" would be bad for him.

Some modern women refuse to be hampered by such taboos. They put up with the soup for a week or so, then get a conniving friend to smuggle fresh fruit into the house.

Malay babies have their heads ceremonially shaved when they are forty days old, at the time the mother's confinement ends. Some are also taught to "tread the ground" at this age. Of course, they are far too small to walk so tiny feet are made to touch the ground, or a handful of earth is carefully held against pink soles.

Whenever possible, a Malay baby is breastfed as it is believed that this fosters a strong spiritual bond between mother and child.

45

Above: **Malay children have a carefree childhood.**

Below: **At five or six a Malay boy is to sent to a Koran teacher, to learn Moslem scriptures.**

GROWING UP IN MALAYSIA

Kampung and longhouse children have a carefree childhood, while their fellows on a Chinese farm or in a shophouse are expected to help at home from quite an early age. A Malay or Dayak lad can play by the water with his friends and run home for a snack or a nap when it suits him. His sister helps mother with household chores; he may go fishing and add his catch to the family meal, but nobody tells him to.

Few Malaysian children are told to do much of anything, not even when to go to bed; at all-night parties or ceremonies they are right there, dropping off to sleep in corners or watching the proceedings.

At five or six, a Malay boy is sent to a Koran teacher, to learn Moslem scriptures. He must master Arabic writing, then words, then whole sentences and chapters. A girl, too, is proficient in the art of Koran Reading. Her brother covers his head with a *songkok*, she wears a muslin veil while handling or reading the Book.

A party is held when a boy has completed the Holy Book. He has to give a public recital of his accomplishment, dressed in his best, supervised by proud teachers and parents.

At the age of ten to twelve, after they have completed reading the Koran, Malay boys are circumcised as their religion demands. Circumcision used to be a semi-public event which involved feasting the whole *kampung*. Nowadays the minor operation is performed by a doctor, in the privacy of his surgery. The family may give a meal to celebrate the safe completion of this rite, inviting close relatives only.

Girls are circumcised too, but not in the drastic fashion prevalent in some parts of North Africa. A slight nick, usually administered by the child's mother or the village midwife, satisfies the demands of tradition.

A girl wears a veil over her head when handling or reading the Koran.

COMMON CHILDHOOD TABOOS

A baby may not be praised or called "fat;" this attracts the attention of evil spirits.

It is forbidden to look at a baby through a mirror; he would drown later in life!

Talking to a baby from the head of his cradle would make him cross-eyed.

Small children may not sit on bed pillows; they would get boils on their buttocks if they do.

Whistling in the dark attracts evil spirits.

A child who is learning to write may not eat chicken legs or feet lest his script become crabbed like a chicken's scratchings.

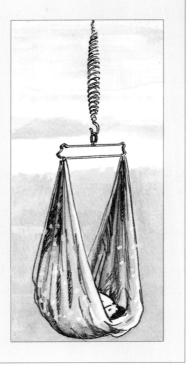

In Malaysian schools, classes are fairly large, about 50 pupils to a class, and discipline is strict. Many schools run two sessions with half the school population attending classes in the morning and the other half, in the afternoon. This maximizes use of limited facilities.

GOING TO SCHOOL

Malaysians start primary school at the age of six. Classes are fairly large and discipline strict. Each child sits at his desk except when "activities" are held. He has to learn a lot of things by heart.

Schoolchildren wear uniform. There will be trouble if girls wear jewelry or make-up, hair-ribbons in any but the regulation colors (navy blue for primary and turquoise for secondary pupils), colorful socks or shoes!

In most schools, students have to stand up to answer a question. When a teacher enters they rise, chanting: *"Selamat pagi, cikgu!"* (pronounced *chegu*)—"Good morning, teacher!" In rural areas, secondary schools have large boarding houses for students who live far away. They only go home for holidays. Some girls in rural areas opt to stay at home after they have completed primary school rather than leave their mothers for boarding school, or old-fashioned parents may refuse their daughters permission to go! The reason given is that the girl needs to learn housekeeping, rather than trigonometry, to prepare her for her future role as wife and mother.

WOMEN AT HOME—MAMA POWER

Within an ordinary Malaysian household, mama rules supreme. She is the first to say that papa is the Head of the Family—outside the home. He makes the big family decisions, he buys the car, he owns the house, but nobody disputes mama's executive powers indoors.

Mama handles the family finances; she decides on how much can be spent on education, what is the best career for a child, where to invest savings. She probably decides how much money papa can spend on the car he proudly buys and owns. Mama is informed about a grown-up son's marriage plans before papa.

This may come as a surprise to people who have heard of timid, servile eastern women and of the East's preference for male babies.

To be sure, while Malaysian women are powerful within their family, they have yet to make an impact on the nation's public life. There are at present only two women ministers and three women deputy ministers in the Federal Cabinet. Women are not represented in many state legislatures.

Women have theoretically equal rights with men, equal access to education and employment. In practice, families with limited funds spend them on their sons, who will have to work for a living one day. Daughters will be supported by their future husbands...or so parents hope.

A large number of married women work in low-paid jobs to supplement a meager family budget. Do they insist that their daughters be educated as carefully as their sons, to increase the girls' future earning power? Unfortunately this is seldom the case. As anybody knows, daughters will be supported by their future husbands...

COURTSHIP—OLD AND MODERN STYLE

A person over 21 is free to choose a marriage partner. But how do Malaysians find one?

Few teenagers in town own cars; group outings by bus are more common than twosome dates. But by the time they attend college, many have paired off, and are beginning to think about marriage.

Town and country tolerate different levels of dating behavior. Kissing in public is out of the question. A young couple walking hand-in-hand in town may attract the occasional frown from passersby; in a seaside *kampung* such displays of abandoned passion would not be permitted.

Many rural girls are betrothed at infancy and may be "married off" by the family at as young as fifteen. "If she does well in school, she'll go to college. If she fails the exams, she'll get married."

Some Indian families obtain spouses for their children from India. A matchmaker draws up horoscopes of possible partners, also considering social and economic position and family history. A bit of a gamble? Happily married middle-aged couples admit they never met before their wedding day.

A bride is expected to be a virgin; conservative in-laws can make her life unpleasant if she is not. The Double Standard reigns supreme; premarital restraint is not seriously expected of young men.

Young people seldom go on single dates, but meet in groups at hamburger bars.

MARRIAGE

Among people of the same race and religion, marriage ceremonies still vary from region to region. Those listed below are the most common in all parts of Malaysia.

MALAY WEDDING Even if a young man has chosen her, his parents have to "obtain" his bride for him. Senior relatives visit the house to inquire whether the young lady is still free. If the reply is encouraging they fix a day for the betrothal, and agree on the dowry and money for the wedding expenses to be given.

The girl is informed by her mother that she is to become a bride. She must act surprised even if the man is her heart's choice! On the other hand, few girls nowadays would marry a man they do not like just because their parents have accepted him.

The engagement may be held several months before the wedding, or on the previous day. It is announced to make a family agreement public.

The essential part of Moslem marriage is the bridegroom's declaration, before mosque officials and other witnesses, to his new father-in-law. After he has performed this to everyone's satisfaction—he may be made to repeat it if it was not loud enough—he is taken to "sit in state" beside his bride.

Gorgeously arrayed, bride and groom sit side by side on decorated chairs. The wedding guests come forward to congratulate and bless them by sprinkling rose water, rice grains and sandalwood paste on the couple's hands. This is called the *bersanding*, and concludes the Moslem wedding ceremonies.

REGIONAL MALAY WEDDING CUSTOMS

The engagement ring is placed on a finger of the bride's right hand by an elder female relative of the groom.

A few weeks before the wedding, an accepted suitor spends a night at his bride's home. After he has left, the lady and her sisters search for gifts of gold hidden among the bedding of the room he slept in.

One day before the wedding, bride and groom have their hands and feet stained red with henna; the bride's hair is trimmed by an elderly female attendant called "Mak Andam."

The bridegroom is denied entry into the bride's house by a champion; his retainer has to "fight" up the steps. The Best Man "bribes" the women of the household to permit the groom access to the inner rooms.

After the *bersanding*, the bride and groom have to feed each other morsels of sweetened rice. This is hilariously messy, but with Mak Andam's help they manage and the wedding feast can begin.

The morning after the wedding the couple is made to sit on the back steps; water is poured over them through a cloth. In the southern State of Johor this leads to a free-for-all splashing party.

CHINESE WEDDING The splendid old-fashioned wedding ceremonies of the Malaysian Chinese are museum pieces today. Many Chinese are Christians now and marry in church. Others opt for marriage at the clan temple or the Registry Office.

One tradition still going strong is the "engagement sweet." The girl's parents order large quantities of a special sweet which is packed in red paper, labeled with the engaged couple's names, and sent to all relatives and friends to announce the forthcoming wedding.

Red paper plays a prominent part in all Chinese weddings, traditional, church or Registry—the invitations are printed on red cards, and guests will bring a present of money in a red envelope. Red signifies luck.

Even modern families observe some old-fashioned customs, the most important being the tea ceremony in which the bride offers tea to her parents-in-law. Acceptance of the tea offered is acceptance of the daughter-in-law into the family.

At the tea ceremony, the bride and groom first offer tea to the groom's parents, and then to elders of the family including uncles, aunts and older siblings of the groom.

Other customs are observed "for the fun of it." One such tradition is that only the bride's younger brother can open the groom's car door. When the groom arrives the boy cannot be found and has to be noisily searched for; then he proves clumsy with the car door handle. A showily administered bribe (wrapped in red paper) suddenly improves his skills, and he lets future Elder Brother-in-law out of the car with many respectful bows.

HINDU WEDDING Three essential ceremonies mark a Hindu wedding: a sacred pipul tree is symbolically planted for the couple by married women; the bride's father puts his daughter's hand into the bridegroom's to give her away; and the young man fixes a gold *thali* pendant, equivalent of a wedding ring, around the woman's neck to make her legally his wife.

The newly married couple then paces seven times around a flame sacred to the fire god Agni. Her veil is attached to his sash to symbolize "the knot has been tied." The officiating priest offers butter, rice and flowers into the fire.

The morning after the wedding, the young husband stains the parting of his wife's hair with vermilion powder in token of her new status. She must wear gold earrings, necklaces, bangles and rings from now on—only a widow goes unadorned.

SIKH WEDDING In former days the Sikh bride used to be wrapped in white cloth, and carried into the groom's presence by her brothers. The modern bride walks, suitably escorted; she wears a red and gold *salwar-kameez* trouser suit and a veil, her groom a western-style suit.

The bride and groom take their vows in front of the Holy Book, surrounded by family and friends. To conclude the ceremony, the groom leads the bride around the Holy Book four times.

Traditionally, the first time a Hindu couple meets is at the wedding. In modern day Malaysia they not only knew but most likely chose each other beforehand.

WORKING LIFE

Young people start to look for work after nine, eleven or thirteen years at school. Unemployment in Malaysia hovers around 5%.

Office jobs are sought by thousands of girls who have taken a typing course; young men like to work in a "company," preferably indoors. There is a strong preference for "eating a government wage" (taking a government job).

Just over 2% of all primary school entrants eventually make it to university, and about the same number graduate from technical or teachers' colleges. Malaysians are eager to educate their children to the highest possible standard, but places in institutions of higher learning are limited and competition is keen.

A young wife usually works after marriage. Once babies begin to arrive, she has to decide whether to continue work, or stay at home and mind the little ones. Many families can rely on a grandmother, an aunt or other relatives to help mind baby, but not all. Day care facilities at the workplace are not common.

The "baby minder" or servant is an important member of many Malaysian families. For the children, she takes the place of the mother, who works outside the home.

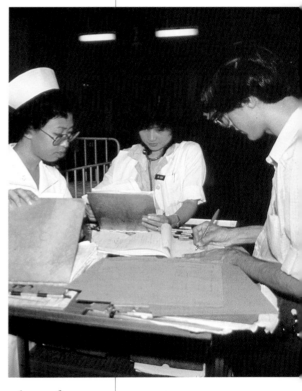

Increasingly, young people are moving away from farms, plantations and small towns into the cities, in search of better jobs, better money, a better life.

HAVING FUN

Malaysians like to get together in large numbers to enjoy festivals and public occasions. It is warm enough all the year round, everything can be celebrated outdoors—just watch for the rain!

Malaysians like to go picnicking in large groups, suitably reinforced by guitars, portable radios and tape players. A picnic party travels to the seaside or a mountain stream by bus. Nature is all very well but Malaysians like it diluted by lots of friends.

The videotape is as triumphant here as elsewhere on earth, but it has not managed to put the neighborhood movie theater out of business. Malaysians like to be in a crowd; grannies, babies, all are taken along to see the latest movie. Young couples find the comparative privacy of a movie theater more romantic than watching the same movie on the video screen at home, surrounded by keenly observant little brothers!

Sports matches never fail to attract huge crowds. To secure good seats, spectators arrive hours early. They can be sure of hundreds of little food and drinks stalls surrounding the stadium, permitting the teams' supporters to combine a picnic with a sports event! Malaysia's favorite sport is soccer, but basketball, tennis, badminton, and recently rugby, have their devoted followings.

Temple occasions, a god's birthday for instance, are celebrated with a procession that instantly collects a crowd. Ritual fire-walkers and sword-swallowers never lack an audience, any more than a cockfight, a quack medicine seller or a traffic accident does.

RICH AND POOR

Malaysia is a country blessed with fertile soils, a balmy climate, rich natural resources and internal peace. Yet there are a surprising number of poor people.

The official figure for Malaysians living below the poverty line is decreasing, but still it stands at 18.4% nationwide (1984). In Sabah and Sarawak it is 33.1% and 31.9% respectively.

The most impoverished groups are rice farmers, fishermen and smallholding agriculturalists. As most rural people get some sustenance directly from their work, maybe the picture is not quite so bad!

Rural poverty stands at 24.7%, however, as opposed to urban poverty, at 8.2%. Farmers' sons drift into town in search of jobs; they hope to "better themselves."

Child beggars who are spotted by the authorities are more fortunate than those who are not.

Beggars in Malaysian towns have, strangely, not much to do with this picture. A good number of them are handicapped. A blind beggar near the mosque door is there to receive alms from the faithful as they go to prayers.

In larger towns there is the *jaga kereta*, "car-minder," who does not mind parked cars but threatens to scratch them unless the owners give him an adequate tip!

If they do not trouble anyone, beggars are tolerated. An exception are child beggars, forced to beg by "owners" who may have bought them from the parents. Such children are placed in orphanages by the welfare authorities.

DEATH RITES

When someone dies, as many family members as possible congregate in the bereaved household. However, the climate dictates that the dead be disposed of as soon as possible, so not everyone can make it on time for the funeral. Many cultures observe rites on certain days after the funeral so that latecomers are able to pay their respects then.

A Moslem cemetery where simple head-stones mark the graves.

MOSLEM Moslems immediately inform the local mosque officials when somebody has passed away—the word "died" is avoided by most Malaysians. The body is washed and shrouded. Only the face is left free and covered with a fine muslin cloth, which relatives may reverently lift for one last look. Until the funeral, which usually takes place on the next day, family and friends keep vigil.

Before burial the body is fully shrouded, placed on a bier or in a coffin and taken to the cemetery. Family members have dug the grave; the body is taken out of the coffin and gently placed in the earth. The call to prayer is recited in the deceased's ear, after which the grave is filled in.

A religious official, protected by an umbrella, recites prayers over the new grave. Flowers, sandalwood shavings and water are strewn over the raw earth.

Orthodox Islam disapproves of tombstones. In Malaysia, however, hardwood or stone grave markers are common and inscribed headstones not unknown.

CHINESE Wealthy Chinese spend a lot of money on a "respectable" funeral. Economy at such a time would be severely criticized by relatives and friends.

A traditional Chinese coffin is hewn out of one trunk of hardwood, a very expensive receptacle. The body is wrapped in many layers of silk gauze and placed in the coffin. Once the heavy coffin is sealed it may be kept in the house for several days until all preparations are ready.

Buddhist monks are invited to chant hymns, and members of the deceased's clan association or relatives serve tea to mourners, keep a record of gifts presented and generally act as undertakers.

The funeral procession leaves the house at a predetermined time, often 2 p.m. Direct descendants are dressed in shapeless garments of unbleached calico or indigo cotton. The cortege is supposed to walk to the burial ground. If it is more than a mile off, the bereaved family arranges for buses to transport the mourners from a certain point along the route.

At the cemetery, the bereaved family presents each person with a new handkerchief which has a red thread sewn into a corner; upon leaving the graveyard this cloth should be waved over one shoulder so spirits cannot follow the departing mourners.

Sometimes, wealthy Chinese engage young male singers whose high-pitched voices are perfect for the elegiac funeral songs.

INDIAN Sikhs and some non-Moslem Indians cremate their dead. This used to be done on an open-air funeral pyre, where tradition demanded that the deceased's son or other close male relative light the fire. Modern crematoria are now available in Malaysia's main towns.

RELIGION

MANY FAITHS

MALAYSIA is a land of many cultures and many faiths which add sound and color to daily life.

Animism is the oldest, and most primitive, religion. The object of worship is Nature: plants, animals, natural phenomena like the weather, all are imbued with spirits which the devotee venerates. Interior tribes of Peninsular Malaysia, the Orang Asli, and some tribal groups in Borneo are animists, or were so until quite recently.

Hinduism, Buddhism and Islam reached Malaysia from India and China. In the early days of the Melaka kingdom, the court was influenced by Hindu beliefs.

Islam is generally thought to have arrived in Melaka in the 15th century, though recent discoveries may push that date back significantly.

The first Christian church in Malaysia was built by the Portuguese in Melaka. More Christian missionaries arrived in the late 19th century. They never attempted to convert the Moslem Malays, but devoted their labors to "pagans" instead.

Above: **The discovery of the Trengganu Stone, which is inscribed with** *jawi* **script, suggests that Islam had arrived in Terengganu by 1303.**

Opposite: **The oldest mosque in Kuala Lumpur, Masjid Jamek, was built in 1909 in the style of northern Indian mosques.**

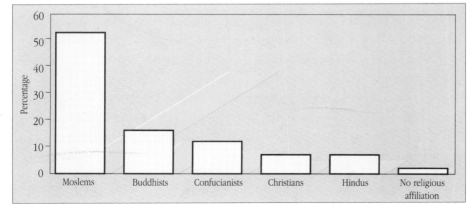

ISLAM

Islam is a Middle Eastern religion based on the revelations of Prophet Mohammed in the 7th century A.D.

A Moslem is obliged to confess his faith, to pray five times daily, to pay a tithe of his income to the mosque, to fast during the month of Ramadan, and to make a pilgrimage to Mecca once in his lifetime.

The earliest prayer, *subuh*, is at about 5.45 to 6 a.m. to coincide with the first blush of dawn. The *zuhur* hour is at noon, *asar* at 4 p.m., *maghrib* at dush and *isyak* after dark. Not every Moslem observes all the hours of prayer, but they are heard from the tower or verandah of mosques and *surau*. Sung by a gifted cantor in the old days, prayers are recordings, replayed and amplified, nowadays.

Moslems wash their faces, hands and feet before prayer, and put on special clothes. Men wear long sleeves, long trousers or a cotton *sarung* and cover their heads with a *songkok* or, if they have performed the pilgrimage, a flat white cap. Women drape a voluminous garment around themselves either to go to the mosque or when praying at home.

One month of the Moslem calendar is devoted to ritual fasting, called *puasa* in Malaysia. No food may be consumed from before dawn till after dark. Night is turned into day with a "breakfast" after the evening prayer, a dinner at midnight and a sustaining pre-dawn meal before *subuh* prayers.

In the days of sailing ships, the Fifth Pillar of Islam, the pilgrimage, was a momentous undertaking. Not many men, and very few women, ever saw the Holy Places. The Malaysian Government encourages Moslems to undertake the pilgrimage nowadays. Through a savings plan, people can accumulate the necessary funds; the trip is organized for them by a Pilgrimage Board.

Mosques and *surau* are places of prayer as well as meeting. They are very plainly furnished. The congregation sits or kneels on the floor, each man on his own prayer rug. There is a lectern and a bookstand holding the Koran, in a niche facing the Holy Land. There are no holy pictures or statues inside a mosque, or anywhere else in a Moslem household, as these would be "images," strictly forbidden by Islam.

HINDUISM

The Indus valley civilization dates back to three millennia B.C.; aspects of Hindu religion are equally ancient.

Hindus revere a pantheon of gods, including the Lord Shiva who rides on a bull and his consort Durga who bestrides a tiger. The august couple symbolize creation, preservation and destruction. The main feature of Hindu religion is that there is no compulsion. Pious Hindus have a little shrine in the house where lamps are lit and offerings of flowers and fruit are made daily, but no divine wrath threatens if this ritual is omitted. People go to the temple as and when it suits them, not because it is the holy day of the week.

By living a good life, a Hindu can ensure that he will be reincarnated as a good person in his next life. A miscreant may be born as a low animal or an insect! Hindus may consult an elaborate horoscope before taking important decisions; a religious man will interpret it.

Malaysian Indians celebrate a number of festivals, among them Deepavali, which traditionally marks the end of the business year among some communities. The house is cleaned and the family decked out in their best clothes. Deepavali means festival of light, and at dusk, house and garden are dotted with candles and twinkling oil lamps.

Celebrating Deepavali at a temple. Deepavali is celebrated by Hindus of all sects to symbolize the triumph of good over evil. There are many legends explaining the origins of the festival; one oft-told tale is how Lord Krishna killed the tyrannical King Naraka-sura in answer to the prayers of his oppressed subjects.

TAOISM, CONFUCIANISM AND BUDDHISM

Most Chinese would say they are "Buddhists" or "Confucianists" without any elaboration. The picturesque Chinese temples hold figurines of various gods and often a Buddha as well, but are not strictly speaking Buddhist.

Buddhism and Confucianism appeal to the intellect. A popular version of Taoism is considered the "religion of the masses." It venerates a multitude of gods, each with his or her own powers. Gods are simpler to grasp than the refinements of Buddhist philosophy. Regional and local gods, provincial heroes deified, and worthy ancestors hold a place in the Chinese temple.

The Chinese who migrated to Malaysia over the centuries brought along their own gods and learned men, the Confucian scholars. The village temple was often the site of the local school and the temple committee was also the school committee.

Temple festivals are calculated according to the lunar calendar. The beginning of New Moon is usually a festival, celebrated with lighting incense sticks or burning "hell money" in big-bellied incinerators. "Hell money" are banknotes of huge denominations, sold for a few dollars per bundle, which mortals use to pay celestial debts.

CHRISTIANITY

The first Christian churches in Malaysia were built in Melaka after 1511 by the Portuguese. In 1553, the remains of St. Francis Xavier were temporarily interred in the Cathedral there until they found a permanent resting place in Goa.

The Portuguese cathedral suffered the fate of many a pioneering religious edifice: when the Dutch took Melaka in 1641, they converted it to their own, protestant, form of Christianity and renamed it St. Paul's. They added Christ Church to the town's landscape, a blood-red building in the Northern Renaissance style that may still be visited today.

There were Christian churches in Penang too. All of them mostly served the foreign trading community. The Malay inhabitants of the Peninsula remained Moslems.

In the early 19th century there was considerable missionary activity in Sarawak and North Borneo, and today both East Malaysian States have a significant number of Christians. The clergy is no longer "imported" but consists of local priests and pastors. Bishops, Moderators, Officers and Presidents of the Catholic, Anglican, Salvation Army and major Protestant churches are all Malaysians.

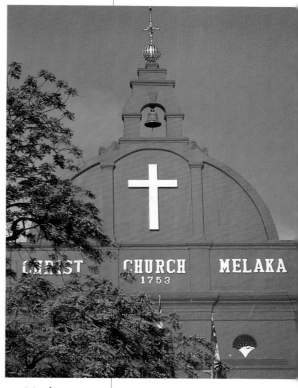

Christ Church in Melaka, a blood-red building in the Northern Renaissance style, built by the Dutch during their rule of Melaka.

ANIMISM

To an animist, all nature is god. Most animists are jungle dwellers, exposed to dangers of climate and accident which they imperfectly understand. If each tree, each plant, each animal, each sound has spiritual meaning, "bad luck" is caused by the anger of one of the many gods.

Animists in the Malay Peninsula and Borneo worshiped large trees. Their farming method forced them to clear jungle every year. This was never done without elaborate ritual to inform the wood spirits. Offerings were placed on the stump of the first tree felled.

Jungle clearing, house building or other communal activities were never undertaken by some tribes without consulting the spirits of the jungle in the form of omen birds.

An insect calling under the house can be a messenger from the underworld. A python crawling into the Orang Asli's jungle shelter can be the personification of a recently deceased family member and must not be chased away. Luckily the python is not a poisonous snake!

Responsibility for bad luck can be conveniently shifted from man to the spirits. A farmer who hurts himself with his ax while felling trees is not careless or clumsy; he must have unknowingly offended any one of the thousands of minor forest deities, forgotten some part of taboo or ritual. His wound is just as painful, but the mishap was not directly his fault!

WHY THE IBAN OF SARAWAK LISTEN TO OMEN BIRDS

(as told by Manang Jabing of Rimbas)

"We Iban are not as ignorant as you may think. We too had writing once upon a time, but it was lost.

Long, long ago there was a huge flood. All the world's people had to run and swim for it. The European put a page of his writing into his hat; the Chinese stuffed a sheet of his letters into the breast pocket of his shirt. But our ancestor had neither hat nor shirt; he put his writing into the back of his loincloth and swam for his life.

Later they met on high land. The European took the paper out of his hat. It was dry, anybody could read it. The Chinese took the paper out of his pocket. It had got wet and the ink was running, that's why Chinese writing looks so squiggly and nobody else can read it.

The Iban took his paper out of his waistband. It was wet too, so he spread it out on a low bush to dry. Then he went off to the jungle to look for a little hunting; the flood had made him hungry.

When he came back to retrieve his writing, the sheet was gone. Birds had eaten it.

They have eaten all our ancestor's wisdom. No wonder the birds are so wise! If we want to know when to start a farm, to build a house, to go hunting or fishing, we ask the birds. They've got the writing—they can tell us."

SUPERSTITIONS

Chinese-speaking Malaysians have many superstitions attached to numbers. Depending on what dialect they speak, a number may mean something that is considered important.

The number eight sounds like "prosperity" in Mandarin and Cantonese, making August 8, 1988, 8.8.88, one of the luckiest days of the century. Droves of couples got married on that date, convinced that conjugal bliss could not fail. Lacking feedback, it is impossible to say whether they all lived happily ever after.

"Prosper and grow, prosper and grow" is what the number of this car sounds like in Cantonese. The Chinese, particularly businessmen, willingly pay premium prices for number plates like this one.

Hokkien speakers pronounce the number four like the word for "death," *si*. Car owners are likely to object if their license plate contains such an unlucky digit. Picture the indignation of the Penang gentleman who was given the car license number "PAK-4!" Pronounced *pak si*, this means roughly: "Drop dead!"

Many superstitions relate to birth and death. Pregnant women are not allowed to attend funerals, and they are carefully protected from ghosts and vampires.

Few Malaysians go to a graveyard without good reason, and a body kept in the house prior to burial is carefully watched; if a cat jumped over it, it would sit up as a ghoul.

Abandoned houses, dark trees and tombs may be haunted. The two rules of thumb regarding these are: keep away from such places; or approach them and wrest a lucky omen from the resident ghost.

STRONG FOLK BELIEF IN MAGIC

When directly asked, most educated Malaysians claim not to be superstitious.

On the other hand, magicians, mediums, witch doctors and faith healers of all kinds do a good business.

There is a general belief that while the doctor at the local hospital may be a very good fellow, he can only deal with naturally caused sickness. Penicillin is not much use against an enemy's wicked spells. Only a spell more wicked than the original will deal with that sort of complaint!

The Malay magician, the *bomoh*, specializes in protective magic. Some States retain a *bomoh* to keep the weather fine during open-air festivities.

Many *kampung* sports teams employ magic to help them win. A *bomoh* blows holy smoke over the team's football boots, or equips them with amulets. If he can get at the field before the match (the Home Team will guard it!) he plants a little charm near the goalposts.

Many children wear magic safeguards in the form of silver capsules, sacred threads, or rattan bracelets. A cross on a little chain is not just a symbol of the wearer's religion but a spell against evil. Non-Christians may sneak into a Catholic church to "borrow" some of the holy water there.

Some magicians perform "black magic" to inflict damage. Evil spirits are called to the black magician's aid. A really bad magician tells an egg to undermine a certain person's health, slowly rot his flesh and dissolve his very bones. The victim must find a stronger *bomoh* who will defuse the spell and send out a stronger one against the original instigator. And so it goes, like the escalation of the arms race!

During the Seventh Month, the ghosts of all persons who died unknown, unmourned or unburied roam the earth. Offerings, joss sticks, hell money and public entertainments mollify them and send them back to where they came from. Nicely treated Hungry Ghosts give little trouble; nobody wants to know how they'd act if they were neglected!

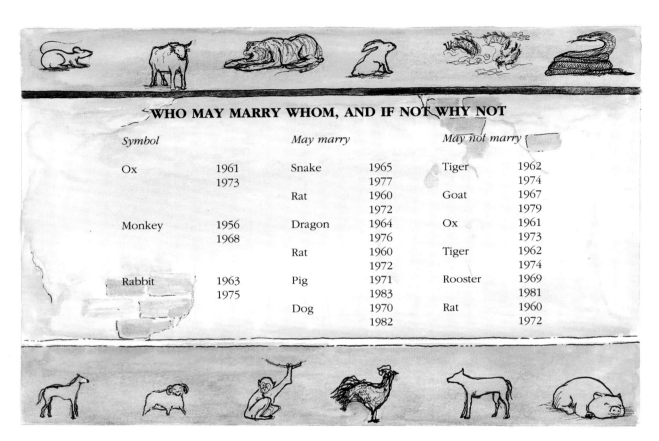

WHO MAY MARRY WHOM, AND IF NOT WHY NOT

Symbol		May marry		May not marry	
Ox	1961	Snake	1965	Tiger	1962
	1973		1977		1974
		Rat	1960	Goat	1967
			1972		1979
Monkey	1956	Dragon	1964	Ox	1961
	1968		1976		1973
		Rat	1960	Tiger	1962
			1972		1974
Rabbit	1963	Pig	1971	Rooster	1969
	1975		1983		1981
		Dog	1970	Rat	1960
			1982		1972

Chinese families are likely to consult horoscopes when a son or daughter is about to be married. The Chinese zodiac has a 12-year cycle, an animal guarding one year in each cycle. Persons of some animal symbols are not supposed to be compatible with others.

ASTROLOGY AND SOOTHSAYING

The revelation that a former U.S. President was interested in astrology may have shocked his own countrymen. It did not ruffle any feathers in Southeast Asia where many statesmen have their personal astrologer. It is understood that a sensible man needs more than human guidance to make important decisions.

When a baby is born, especially an eldest son, Hindu families may ask an astrologer to cast a horoscope for the child's entire life. The very minute of the infant's birth has to be determined, and from there his life will be charted by the stars.

Malaysians like to glimpse into the future by means other than horoscopes, too. One can consult a professional fortuneteller, who may have a name plate outside his door reading: *Tukang Ramal* ("Future Maker"). He has various methods at his command. Palm reading is fairly widespread, but is not the only means.

Some fortunetellers keep a tame animal. Strips of paper are put into its cage and the mouse or hamster will tear them to shreds at once. The client's fortune is predicted from scraps that fall outside the bars.

Many Chinese temples employ a medium who can work himself (or herself) into a trance and tell fortunes by uttering cryptic remarks that must be interpreted by a competent attendant.

The do-it-yourself method is to borrow a bamboo quiver full of long wood or ivory sticks from the temple guardian. The devotee, having offered prayers, incense and suitable gifts, shakes the quiver until one or several sticks fall out. The future may be deciphered by interpreting the inscriptions on the various sticks.

Unlike the gypsy-at-the-fair, fortunetellers and astrologers are respected members of the Malaysian community. While orthodox religions like Islam and Christianity are not entirely at ease with these practices, the general public patronizes astrologers in large numbers. Forewarned is forearmed!

Many fortunetellers set up shop on roadsides or covered walkways outside shophouses.

Almost everyone in Malaysia speaks at least a smattering of Malay, the lingua franca between the different races.

LANGUAGE

MULTILINGUAL COUNTRY

THE OFFICIAL LANGUAGE of Malaysia is Bahasa Malaysia, a standardized form of Malay; "Bahasa" means language.

Malay in its many variants has long been the lingua franca of the Malay Archipelago. From as far north as the Philippines to as far south as New Guinea, traders and locals can communicate in some form of Malay. In the interior of the great islands of Borneo, Sumatra and New Guinea many native tongues are spoken, but the coastal fringe dwellers are often Malays, or natives who can speak a version of it.

"Official language" does not mean Only Language, of course. Malaysia's second largest racial group after the Malays are the Chinese, who make up 7 million of the population and speak Chinese, but this does not mean all understand each other! Dialect variants can be mutually unintelligible and a Chinese may use Mandarin, the Chinese dialect taught in school, Malay or even English to talk to a person from another Chinese community. The main Chinese dialects spoken in Malaysia are Mandarin, Cantonese, Hakka, Teochew and Hainanese. The Indian community of 1.5 million is also divided up into lingual units: Tamil, Telugu, Punjabi, Hindi, Gujarati and Urdu are spoken here.

East Malaysia is the land of the "small" languages, some used by just a few thousand people; rugged terrain and inter-tribal warfare isolated people from each other. Some Sarawak languages are Iban, Bidayuh, Melanau, Kayan, Kenyah, Kelabit, Lun Bawang and Lun Dayeh. In Sabah one might hear Rungus, Kadazan, Murut, Bisaya, Bajau, Illanun and Suluk.

While Bahasa Malaysia is used in all the country's schools as the sole medium of instruction, some government-run schools teach a few classes a week in the pupil's own language; this applies mainly to Chinese and Tamil or mixed communities.

In most parts of the country, the Chinese communities insist on the right to educate their young in the mother tongue. They are allowed to do this, but the syllabus is carefully structured to ensure sufficient instruction in Bahasa Malaysia.

NEWSPAPERS IN MALAYSIA

Not all Malaysians are literate, but those who can make sense of a printed page will spend some time each day poring over a newspaper.

Newspapers come in a variety of languages including Bahasa Malaysia, English, Chinese, Tamil, Punjabi, Malayalam and Kadazan. The majority of these newspapers are printed in roman script, the same as this book. However, some languages have their own scripts.

Malay has no script of its own. Islamic missionaries brought with them the Holy Book and a system of writing which can be used to transcribe Malay quite accurately. The Arabic script, known as *jawi* here, is still used for some religious and formal purposes. When Europeans first began to travel and trade in the region, they recorded what names and technical terms interested them in a rough and ready fashion. Depending on whether the scribe was Portuguese, Dutch or English, he would write "Suraia," "Soeraja" or "Sooraya" for the same name. Over the years a generally accepted romanized system has crystallized. Malay newspapers are either printed in *jawi* or romanized Malay.

Chinese is written in ideograms. Each character stands for an idea or a combination of ideas. A "simplified" version of written Chinese, used among other things for printing newspapers, contains 2,500 to 3,000 characters.

Indian languages like Tamil, Urdu and Malayalam are written in scripts of their own.

Newspapers come in two sizes—tabloid and broadsheet—and in many languages! There are 4 dailies and 8 weeklies in Bahasa Malaysia, 8 dailies and 4 weeklies in English, 16 dailies and 10 weeklies in Chinese, 3 dailies in Tamil and 1 daily each in Punjabi, Malayalam and Bahasa/English/Kadazan.

BAHASA MALAYSIA

Bahasa Malaysia is, in a way, a synthetic language: it is a standardized form of the dialect variants of the Malay language. Schoolchildren occasionally have difficulty in distinguishing between "proper" language and the form they speak at home. The two are nearly the same, but not quite.

People of the various regions speak dialects of their own. Some dialects vary in stress patterns and speech rhythms, others in vocabulary. A Malay farmer from Johor would have to listen very carefully to understand what another Malay farmer from Terengganu is telling him. Both would stare at what a Malay colleague from Sabah tries to contribute to the conversation—yet all three speak Malay.

Standard Bahasa Malaysia is the language heard on radio and television, and taught in schools. The spelling has been standardized to make it more or less compatible with Bahasa Indonesia, another form of Malay spoken by about 100 million Indonesians. Vocabulary is also being standardized and constantly revised. An educated Indonesian could understand an educated Malaysian even though there are a few minor differences between their languages.

After all, an educated American, a Canadian and a Briton can choose to understand each other perfectly, or pretend to have great difficulty with the others' "barbaric" lingo.

On television, when a non-Malay language program is shown, it is invariably accompanied by Malay subtitles.

DO-IT-YOURSELF

A simple pronunciation guide is that all Malay vowels are the same as in Italian—*a* as in father, *e* as in pet, *i* as in pit, *o* as in pot, and *u* as in put.

Good morning!
Selamat pagi!

What's new with you?
Apa khabar?

Everything's fine, thank you.
Biasa sahaja, terima kasih.

My name is Jamil.
Nama saya Jamil.

What's your name?
Siapa nama anda?

Are you from America?
Anda datang dari Amerika?

I am from Malaysia, from Kampung Hilir Sungei.
Saya datang dari Malaysia, dari Kampung Hilir Sungei.

Malaysia is a hot country, but it rains a lot.
Negeri Malaysia panas tetapi selalu hujan.

Come with me to Kampung Hilir Sungei.
Mari ikut saya Kampung Hilir Sungei!

My father's house is not very big.
Rumah ayah saya tidak berapa besar.

Come up to the house!
Sila naik ke rumah!

Please take off your shoes; this is our custom.
Sila buka kasut anda, inilah adat resam kami.

Sit here, please. My younger sister will bring a cool drink.
Sila duduk di sini. Nanti adik saya akan membawa minuman segar.

BODY LANGUAGE

Verbal language is not always essential to communication. A shake of the head means "no" in most parts of the world, a smile and nod "yes." In Malaysia, some gestures are peculiar to an ethnic group while some are common to all. For instance, it is generally not considered polite to point at persons or things with the index finger. A bent index finger or thumb is used to point, in effect, "knuckle," in the right direction.

Malaysians do not touch each other unless they are close friends or relatives. In a crowd, a woman holds her dress to herself to avoid touching passersby with it.

Moslems greet each other by touching each other's right hand and then their own chests. This is the *salam,* a gesture meaning "I greet you from my heart." It may be done with both hands to show greater deference, especially with older people.

Moslems greet each other by just touching each other's right hand and then their own chests, and conservative Moslem women will not shake hands with a man, but bow gently. The old-fashioned Chinese way of greeting, shaking one's clasped hands, waist-high, while bowing, is used only by the older Chinese these days. Similarly, the Indian palm-to-palm greeting, or *namaskar*, is used only on ceremonial occasions now. On the other hand, the western handshake is increasingly used as a form of greeting, especially in the business community. Among friends, Sikh men like to go in for the back-slapping, pummeling style of welcome.

In courtship, the language of sighs and glances is used: a young lady's seemingly innocent offer of a quid of betel* to a young man, a dropped lace handkerchief left where he is sure to find it.

Language—who needs it?

* Parings of betel nut with a dash of lime are wrapped in a betel leaf, and then chewed for enjoyment.

A *pantun* contest held by the national television station.

CONTEST OF WORDS

Malaysians respect an articulate, confident speaker. The children's early training in reciting the Koran before an audience is often given as an example of early preparation for public speech.

One of the entertainments at an old-fashioned party was *pantun*. This was originally a Malay pastime but others, especially the Straits Chinese, have learned this game and made it their own. The men at a party compose four-liners, often humorous in content, to challenge the women. One of the women's side is called upon to answer, and her reply usually has the necessary sting. Another man speaks up for his gender, another woman rebuts him—this merry exchange goes on until dawn, and is by no means confined to the young. You do not learn to improvise well until you have seen a few birthdays!

Pantun do not have to be ribald— tender sentiment can be expressed through this medium too. But, recited as they are in front of a festive crowd, the message has to be carefully veiled.

Kalau tuan mudik ke hulu
Carikan sahaya bunga kemoja
Kalau tuan mati dahulu
Nantikan sahaya di pintu syurga.

Should you travel upstream
find me a sweet-scented flower
Should you die before I do
wait for me at heaven's gates.

THE BROADCAST MEDIA

Broadcasting only hit Peninsular Malaysia in 1946 and East Malaysia in the 1950s. Television was introduced in 1963, and extended to East Malaysia in 1972. Most programs are in Bahasa Malaysia, with air time for Chinese and Indian dialects, and regional languages in East Malaysia. States have their own radio studios.

A musical gala, organized jointly by Malaysia's RTM and TV Indonesia and aired "live" in both countries.

TV, especially TV advertising, has done a lot to mold the tastes and ideas of Malaysia's young people. However remote their village, if there is electricity there will be at least one TV set. They have the tastes and habits of the moneyed middle class displayed before their dazzled eyes. Most of them want to get to a big town to see the glamor promised by the consumption-oriented media.

Oral tradition wilts before the onslaught of electronic sound. Excellent cultural programs show the best traditional performers. The immediate reaction of a *kampung*-renowned specialist is: "This is a lot better than I can do. I should lose face if I sang this song again!" The prospective audience may not urge the village star to put on his act anyway. They are busy watching TV!

In remote areas, the radio may be the community's only immediate link with the outside world. Forty-five news bulletins are broadcast daily from the national station. Regional stations repeat them in local dialects.

Mak Yong, a traditional Kelantanese dance, was once performed to amuse the Sultan's womenfolk.

THE ARTS

TRADITIONAL LITERATURE

THERE SEEMS TO BE no form of primitive, traditional Malaysian drama. The best-known dramatic arts are imports: *wayang kulit* and *bangsawan* from Indonesia, Chinese opera from China.

To make up for it, there is an impressive body of traditional literature. Some of it is based on oral sources, only written down in the 19th century; some, especially East Malaysian tribal literature, remains unrecorded to this day.

Cycles of sagas in which fact and legend blend are known in every State. The stirring tales of Admiral Hang Tuah and his noble fellows make good hearing or reading to this day. The history of Malaya has been recorded in the *Sejarah Melayu*, the *Malay Annals*. The narrative starts somewhat grandiloquently with Alexander the Great, who is described as the ancestor of Malay royalty, but it gets down to brass tacks by about the 14th or 15th century. If the doings of the 16th century Sultans are not uniformly edifying, they are certainly interesting.

The works of a 19th century Malay author, Munshi Abdullah, are still studied in schools as literature texts. A much-traveled and well educated man, Abdullah wrote several books of travels as well as a story of Malay feudal and social history, the *Kisah Pelayaran Abdullah*.

There are many tales of heroism about the legendary Admiral Hang Tuah of the Melaka Sultanate. But there is one tale of romance which has charmed audiences, and that is how he stole a bride for Sultan Mansur Shah. The lady in question, Tun Tijah of Pahang, was betrothed to the Terengganu Sultan whom she did not love. Hang Tuah traveled to Pahang, and there, charmed Tun Tijah so that she fell in love with him and willingly fled with him to Melaka. On the way, Hang Tuah broke the charm so that the lady later fell in love with the handsome Sultan of Melaka.

DANCE

Traditional dances are popular, but few Malaysians learn them thoroughly. Schoolgirls go through the motions of *Bunga Melur*, or learn dances set to Chinese tunes.

To first-timers, East Malaysian dance looks tortuous. Parties fill a longhouse with guests to almost bursting point. A dance of vigorous leaps and bounds might just prove too much for the building!

Those who dance seriously face hard training, like the western ballerina. Stress is laid on supple hands: a classical Malay dancer can bend her fingers back to almost touch her forearm!

MAK YONG *Mak Yong* is a dance of Kelantan set to traditional music. The violin whines the tune, bossed gongs and skin drums throb a rhythm of mesmerizing monotony.

After the stage has been cleansed, gorgeously costumed dancers enter. The male lead, Pak Yong, is good-looking to the point of pretty—for good reason: "he" is danced by a girl, as are all male characters except one aged clown.

Mak Yong used to be organized to amuse the Sultan's womenfolk. Handsome young men could not perform in the harem! The clown was old enough to be "trustworthy" and many of his lines are ribald hints to this fact.

EAST MALAYSIAN DANCES East Malaysians have preserved many of their people's traditional dances. Dayak children are taught dancing at an early age. The slow, complicated movements require excellent muscle control. Dancing is supposed to make boys agile and girls graceful.

MALAY DANCE Some old Malay dances have been adapted to modern usage. *Ronggeng* and *joget,* traditionally danced by men only as an audience entertainment, are performed as "mixed doubles" on the dance floor nowadays. The decencies must be preserved, of course—throughout the fairly intricate gyrations of a *ronggeng,* the couple never touch each other. Their bodies and arms make reciprocal movements, hands almost but never quite touch! To foreign eyes the classical Malay dances have something of a Spanish air, partly due to their common Moorish heritage.

INDIAN DANCE An Indian girl who wants to learn her people's classical dances is advised to start by age five. There are teachers who are prepared to take a student through her early steps, not forgetting initiation prayers before the Lord Shiva, god of dance, at whose altar she must present her jingling anklets.

Basic classical dancing involves about 100 steps and movements, which are choreographed into dance-dramas of old narratives. When the novice reaches her tenth or eleventh year, she is ready to perform, solo, the six major dances of the *Bharathanatyam,* 16th century classical works.

After this display, which is an initiation at the same time, the girl will be able to take her place among the mature dancers in temple ceremonies and public performances.

A teacher taking her young novice through her paces.

MUSIC OF THE MALAY PENINSULA

The original music of the Malay Peninsula is percussive. Long ago large gongs served to send messages from one place to another. They still give the basic beat for many dances. Whole ensembles of gongs, from huge boomers to delicate tinklers, are used in the Javanese *gamelan* orchestra, which is occasionally heard in Malaysia, too.

A Malay gong orchestra.

Besides gongs there are drums. The man-sized "long drums" of the northern part of the Malay Peninsula are made of hollowed tree trunks covered with taut buffalo or goat skin. Small tambourines are an import from the Arab world. These are beaten to keep time to the strident singing of Arab songs which commonly accompany Malay weddings. The Arabs also brought a species of lute with them, the *gambus*, skillfully played by many Malays.

In many villages there is a *keroncong* band, an ensemble playing old-fashioned music on fiddles, hand-drums, small harmonicas and, sometimes, flutes.

Peculiar to the courts of Kedah, Perak, Terengganu and Selangor is the *nobat*, a band consisting of a straight, valveless silver trumpet, a flute, a gong and a consort of drums. The *nobat* only performs on ceremonial occasions such as a ruler's ascension, wedding or funeral. It has a haunting quality. Few who have heard it once can forget the *nobat*.

EAST MALAYSIAN MUSIC

In the past, among the East Malaysians, gongs were considered more than musical instruments. Brought into the country by barter trade, they were symbols of wealth and stability as well. Many old rituals involve the use of gongs: Bidayuh wash their ancestral head trophies in an overturned gong full of coconut water; Iban bridal couples sit on a pair of gongs.

Many reed and bamboo flutes are used in East Malaysia. Some, resembling the "jew's harp," are so soft they can hardly be heard except by someone near the performer. Others are used at ceremonies and parties and can be quite shrill. Flute tunes are usually brief motifs of arpeggios, repeated with minor variations again and again. It is not common for people to sing when wind instruments are being played. Borneo natives also play a mouth-organ with upstanding bamboo pipes, and a gourd that serves as wind chamber.

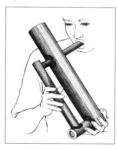

A bamboo bass flute.

A string instrument native to Sabah is the "bamboo zither." A thick bamboo has strips of its skin lifted up; each section is pegged with little wedges to stretch and tune it.

The "wood xylophone" consists of hardwood sticks of varying lengths stretched on a string ladder.

The *jotong utog*, or "wood xylophone."

A string instrument made and played by the Kenyah and Kayan people of central Borneo, the *sape* is made out of a single piece of wood. It has two to four strings. Expert players rearrange the frets for "happy" and "solemn" tunes.

MODERN MUSIC

Much Malaysian patriotic music would sound sentimental to the foreign ear. Love for the nation is expressed in the same swooning tones and words that would be used to woo a maiden, often in tunes strongly reminiscent of Indonesian *keroncong*.

On big occasions, rallies, processions and open-air functions, sentiment would not produce the sound waves required. Malaysia does indeed have brass bands, and they can rival the best when it comes to oom-pah-pah and big drums. Military units, the police, schools, even private firms maintain brass bands of varying quality.

As for modern music, you name it Malaysia has it. Besides obvious copycat efforts like "The Malaysian Elvis Presley," there are excellent indigenous modern bands.

Musical preferences can lead to tense situations among *kampung* youngsters if one village is Heavy Metal and the next is Rock! Nearly every village has its own band, a couple of electric guitars and the required amount of percussion. The amplifiers are always in great shape if nothing else is.

In the bigger towns there are modern dance bands with an ever-changing supply of performers and singers. Malaysia has many talented musicians, and a few each year make it to the top.

VISUAL ART

Malaysia shares with Indonesia the tradition of *batik* wax-resist fabric printing, used to produce fabrics for clothing. In recent years, however, it has also become an accepted artistic medium.

The younger artists branch off from the traditional, Dutch-inspired path trod by Old Masters like Mohammed Hoessein bin Enas, a well-known portrait painter who uses mainly oils. They try abstract renditions of their ideas in modern media like tempera, acrylic and collage.

There are many Art Clubs throughout Malaysia. Members get together for sketching and study sessions, and go for occasional working trips outdoors. Visitors to a popular picnic spot are used to the sight of half a dozen artists perched on as many boulders in the middle of a rushing rapid, serenely sketching on folios balanced on their knees. Nothing but a heavy shower will drive them off their vantage points!

Chinese brush painting is an art form brought here by immigrants, but it is well established. Besides traditional motifs, some painters depict local scenery, fruit, insects and wildlife in the quick fluid brush strokes of their craft.

Batik, the traditional method of wax-resist fabric printing, has become an accepted artistic medium.

PUBLIC SPEAKING AS AN ART

Malaysians of all races value an articulate speaker who can stand up and say his piece at any occasion. There is a body of traditional literature that was orally preserved until the quite recent past; some of it is in danger of being lost because it is still unrecorded.

The traditional pastimes survive to a limited extent in the *kampung* and longhouses of remote areas. They are also enjoying a new lease of life as public entertainment. At official and private functions, it is considered chic to have a recitation of an extract of one of the interminable *syair* stories, or a *Mak Yong* performance.

Schools organize rhetoric and speech contests to encourage students to speak confidently and freely. Rhetoric tends to degenerate into ranting in some cases, but the standard of debating is usually very high. Inter-school debates are "fought" by proper rules in general, with regional variants. A speaker will lose marks for pointing at the opposing side; that's not against Oxford etiquette but it's bad manners in Malaysia.

HANDICRAFT

On the east coast of Peninsular Malaysia, fishing is a main source of income. The people still have the leisure to embellish their boats, necessities of life in a very real sense, to add a splash of color to the scene of long white beach, deep green jungle and dark green sea.

In Sarawak, Borneo's best backstrap loom weavers are to be found. Iban women tie-dye the warp threads of their cotton fabric into intricate traditional patterns. When the cloth is woven the ready-made patterns appear.

Many Malaysian men are woodcarvers who like to beautify articles of daily use with fretwork, whittling or surface incision. The fascia boards of old-fashioned Malay houses are often thus decorated, so are women's weaving utensils, game boards, bed-heads and mirror frames.

Above: **Kite fighting is a sport; kite making is an art. This old gentleman has a lifetime's experience behind him when it comes to cutting, pasting, stringing and properly balancing the frail craft; he paints and decorates it to rival the other villages' best in the coming kite competition.**

Left: **Carving a tall ceremonial post to be erected next to a longhouse.**

Top-spinning is a game not only for teenagers, but grown men as well. On the east coast of Peninsular Malaysia, the local village hero is the champion top-spinner. The top-spinning season begins after the harvest with contests for the longest spinning top or the deadliest striker.

TRADITIONAL GAMES

CONSIDERING THAT MALAYSIA is a very peaceful country, it is amazing how many popular pastimes involve fights of some sort. Besides hopscotch and knucklebones, children play *kuncum*. On the count of *kun-choom!* each makes a hand symbol: scissors, paper or stone. Scissors cut paper, stone damages scissors, paper wraps stone....I win! you lose!

Even kites fight in Malaysia. The line is dipped in gum and then in powdered glass, so it will cut an opponent adrift if skillfully played. Paying out line is a hazardous operation; many "kite fighters" wear one leather glove. Kite flying competitions may be practiced as an inter-village contest, and the champions are grown men.

Spinning tops can be used to fight with, as can quoits, somewhat like pitching horseshoes. An elaborate version of coconut shy involves throwing a coconut half-shell over prizes. If the nut shell covers the item, the contestant can claim it.

Schoolboys have fighting fish in jars and fighting beetles in match boxes. Their elder brothers play a more exciting game that strikes most foreigners as cruel: cockfighting.

Cockfighting is known in all parts of Malaysia. A whole science attaches to the choice of the right bird for the right hour, and the matching of contestants by weight, breed or color. A fancier will pay from US$110 to over US$370 for a pedigree fighting cock. He wins—or loses—several times his pet's value in prizes and bets.

The contest itself is swift and bloody. Razor-sharp blades are tied over the birds' spurs. Two are released into a ring and clash in the center in a flurry of feathers and a spurt of blood. The losing bird is left expiring or dead, or runs out of the ring.

FISHING

Some Malaysians make their living as fishermen. Others wish they may —this, at any rate, explains Malaysians' abiding love for fish and fishing.

Almost every settlement is near a river or the sea. The boat jetty or harbor wall is sure to be populated with fishermen and boys, using a variety of tackle. Urban wage-earners make weekend trips to promising spots such as waterfalls, rapids, a quiet bridge or an old embankment that promises undisturbed communion with the fish.

Many people like to stretch nets across little rivers, or to set traps. A common fish trap looks like a long round basket, with an entry hole defended by tapering rattan rods. A fish can get in but not out; the owner of the trap opens a little hinged door in the side to collect his catch.

The people's well known love for water and fishing has led to a small industry providing modest seaside and riverside huts, elegantly styled "chalets," that are rented out by the day or week. Such shelters are usually very basic, with a sleeping room, cooking facility and some sort of washroom. The rent is paid for the whole unit, the owner does not care how many people are jammed into it for a few days. Families, school classes, clubs, any group that cannot afford to stay at a proper "beach resort" gets all the fun of beach, river or island entertainment at a modest price.

Holiday "chalets" on stilts. The sun, sea and fresh air more than make up for the spartan facilities.

WATER SPORTS

There are beach resorts in Malaysia, and very elegant ones at that. Hotels and clubs on the wide beaches of the east coast of Peninsular Malaysia and Borneo invite the affluent holiday-maker to a vacation of wind-surfing, snorkeling, scuba diving, sailing, or simply lounging on the warm sand.

Food at such establishments is usually of the international hotel-cuisine type, heavy on seafood. Some guests have their own catch cooked for dinner. Knowledgeable tourists, however, wander beyond their hotel. There is sure to be a *kampung* or a bazaar near by. The same lobster, *garoupa*, turtles' eggs or crab is sizzled up here in full view of the hungry consumer, spiced with whatever the regional flavor dictates, sold at a fraction of the hotel price.

Malaysia has the natural advantage of a tropical climate. It can occasionally be too windy or too rainy for much outdoor sport, but it is never too cold. Even during the rainy season, some fine days can be enjoyed by the water.

Scuba diving off the eastern State of Tereng-ganu.

Malaysia's larger towns have their own water-sports clubs. Scuba diving is a new sport fast catching on among the affluent. In the *kampung*, boys may be seen with snorkels and flippers or diving masks, giving the sea and river fish a hard time with their bamboo fishing spears.

LAND SPORTS

BALL GAMES Soccer and cricket caught on like wildfire in the Malaya of the early 20th century. Basketball, table tennis and badminton are popular in present-day Malaysia.

There is also a local sport, somewhat resembling volleyball—*sepak takraw* ("kick the *takraw*-ball").

Originating at the courts of Siam and Melaka, the game used to involve two or more players. They formed a circle, kicking, shouldering and heading a hollow rattan ball between each other without letting it touch the ground. *Kampung* boys still play it this way. Exact rules were drawn up in 1946, and a net was introduced, as well as a proper scoring system. The game was formally included in the Southeast Asia Games in 1965, played by teams from Malaysia, Brunei, Indonesia, Thailand, Burma, Singapore and the Philippines.

A *sepak takraw* team consists of two wings and one back, the *tekong*, who opens the game by kicking the ball across the net. Unlike volleyball, each player can hit the ball three times in succession. The ball may be hit with any part of the body other than the hands or arms, which serve mainly as wings to balance the players' acrobatic leaps and tumbles.

MARTIAL ARTS *Silat* is an old Malay form of self-defense, not unlike shadowboxing. Small boys are taught the basic movements, unarmed. Mock fighting is not encouraged by *silat* masters until the combatants have learned discipline and restraint.

In urban areas, other forms of unarmed defense are popular among the young. Many join *taekwando* classes, kicking their feet over their heads with great gusto.

Older people are sometimes seen in the town's parks, in the cool of dawn, practicing slow, rhythmic movements called *tai-chi*. This very ancient Chinese martial art, now much prized as a form of exercise, is believed to strengthen the body without exhausting or overstraining it.

MALAYSIANS AND MUSIC

A Malay *kampung* has a *kompang* band, an ensemble of boys and girls beating goatskin tambourines, accompanied by the drummers' own singing. A good band can be in demand for weddings and other festive occasions throughout the district.

Chinese music enthusiasts get together to form chamber groups. These dispense with the percussion that gives Chinese opera its deafening resonance, using knee-fiddles, flutes, lutes and sometimes one softly played tambourine.

In towns, formal western music lessons are available. Many middle class children are encouraged to learn piano. Like anywhere else, most "drop out" after a few years, while the few talented performers reach an admirable standard. Malaysian music students take examinations from the Royal School of Music or Trinity College.

Those who do not play, sing. Schoolchildren sing; fishermen sing; soldiers sing; birds' nests collectors sing on the way to their dangerous work in deep caves. Many Malaysians are members of church or secular choirs. Office staff choirs serenade visitors. School choirs are inevitable. Most teenagers go through a feverish stage of trying to rival Michael Jackson or outdo Rick Astley if not Madonna. Luckily the damage is, in most cases, only superficial...

The local *kompang* band, of young boys and girls, is usually present whenever there is a village festivity, adding to the festive mood with its music.

DRAMATIC PURSUITS

Malaysia does not have any indigenous drama. People are very fond of watching a dramatic performance, but until quite recently it was not considered quite the thing for respectable citizens, or their children, to be seen on a stage. "Outsiders" provided the entertainment.

The *bangsawan*, once a traveling show, was something not unlike an operetta. The involved plot was broken by unconnected interludes called "extra turns" which permitted one actor (or actress) to garner a little separate applause and maybe a shower of coins. Stories and music were often improvised by the performers: one *bangsawan* popular before the war was called "Lohengrin and His Big Duck"—Wagner's grand opera adapted to suit a culture where swans are unknown!

The famous Indonesian shadow play, *wayang kulit*, used to be performed by strolling players. Puppets cut out of stiff leather were manipulated with a set of movable sticks behind a white sheet illuminated by a couple of kerosene lanterns. The shadows on the screen told a story from the Hindu classics, dubbed live by the puppet master and his assistants.

Many *bangsawan* performers were children, bought from their parents or shadier sources for this trade. The court books of the prewar period are full of complaints against *bangsawan* masters ill-using their charges, or even kidnapping pretty children before the show moved on to another town!

Chinese opera may be seen from time to time in most Malaysian towns. This is a form of drama with close religious connections; a temple deity's birthday is often celebrated with an opera. The hungry ghosts

which roam the land during the Chinese seventh month are generally appeased with lavish operatic performances.

In Chinese opera, quite young actors may get their early training in silent parts, as attendants or messengers, before graduating to Prince, Emperor, General, Princess or Queen. While the Emperor or the General are always sung by men, the part of the Prince, especially in a romantic work, may be performed by a young woman. The part requires a very high tenor voice and the character is supposed to look "sweet."

One very ancient Malaysian spectator art is storytelling. Especially in the days when hardly anybody could read, before the radio and TV provided entertainment in the long evenings, a practiced storyteller could be sure of an enthralled audience. There is a Malay method of chanting a historical tale, called *syair,* which often entertained choice gatherings at royal parties.

One Sarawak story takes nine nights to tell. Longhouse festivals may involve three or four reciters who walk up and down, up and down the long verandah for up to eight hours without once stopping before their story-song is done!

Today's performers in Chinese opera are often amateurs. There is not enough demand for this entertainment to maintain professional singers and actors. Enthusiasts give up many hours of their free time to practice singing, the intricate stage movements and gestures and the correct management of heavy, cumbersome costumes.

AFTER SCHOOL

One very popular entertainment, especially for school-age youngsters, is wandering around shopping malls. Such expeditions are always undertaken in groups. A bunch of boys here and a bunch of girls there are fully aware of each other. They may very possibly follow each other around, even sit at adjoining tables in the hamburger joint, but no boy would say he had been "out with the girls."

Shopping itself is a secondary consideration to mall-walking. The main thing is meeting friends, gawking at strangers and giggling at the local "freak show" provided by the occasional eccentric or unusually fashionable outfit or hairstyle.

If one of the group has a transistor radio it must be turned on at full volume, regardless of what the shops are already producing by way of decibels.

Movie theaters are popular entertainment spots, as are skating rinks and bowling alleys, all to be visited by a group. One person arriving by him- or herself would feel out of place!

Boys who have them love to ride their motorcycles around town, slow enough for their friends to see, but fast enough to produce noise. After dark, there are illegal motorcycle races on the less frequented roads.

GOLD RUSH SYNDROME

A gregarious lot, Malaysians love to be wherever something is going on. A seemingly innocent notice in a newspaper can spark off mass movement. Reports of the sighting of supernatural signs in a lake, a river, a beach, will draw crowds of sightseers. Hawkers follow the throng. The monster may or may not show up but a good time was had by all who waited for it! A miracle healer may attract a sudden influx of patients to a roadless village, or a spring is discovered to have incredible healing powers. Once a stampede starts it is impossible to stop until it runs out naturally.

Once in a while, a small gold rush breaks out in Malaysia. A farmer finds gold dust or what he considers to be raw diamonds in his fields. Within days the place will be swarming with prospectors armed with large flat pans called *dulang*, used for washing soils to extract the precious mineral. The gold may prove scanty or entirely absent, and the village will return to normal in good time.

The scene of a crime becomes a "sightseeing spot" for the ghoulish part of the public, to the annoyance of the police who are investigating. Gawkers may block the fire engine from reaching a conflagration,…but Malaysians are not unique in that respect, are they?

Zoos, parks and waterfronts are thronged with family groups on a Sunday, as are historical places and the more accessible picnic spots—including the Kota Tinggi waterfalls in Johor.

FESTIVALS

CALENDAR OF FESTIVALS

January/February	Chinese New Year
	Chap Goh Mei
	Thaiponggal
	Thaipusam
April	Hari Raya Puasa
May	Kadazan Harvest Festival*
	Vesak Day
June	Gawai Dayak*
July	Hari Raya Haji
	Ma'al Hijrah
August	National Day*
October	Prophet Mohammed's birthday
	Deepavali
December	Christmas*

* These are the only festivals that fall on the same day each year, according to the Gregorian calendar. The other festivals fall on different days each year because they are fixed according to different calendars. Chinese New Year, Chap Goh Mei and Vesak Day are fixed according to the Chinese lunar calendar while Thaiponggal, Thaipusam and Deepavali are according to the Hindu calendar. Hari Raya Puasa, Hari Raya Haji, Ma'al Hijrah and Prophet Mohammed's birthday are fixed according to the Moslem calendar.

Opposite: **National Day (August 31) in Malaysia means a parade, brass bands, veterans, uniforms, flags, noise, and people, people, people! It is always a school holiday, but no schoolboy would dream of staying at home.**

National Day commemorates the date when the Federation of Malaya came into being in 1957, with the granting of independence by the British.

CHINESE NEW YEAR (January/February)

The New Year is a bit of a problem in Malaysia. Which New Year do you mean—the "ordinary" or "western" New Year, the Chinese New Year, the Moslem New Year, or the Hindu New Year? Each is celebrated by some people, though the Chinese New Year must take the prize for noise and hilarity.

The Chinese New Year marks the beginning of a new lunar year; thus it falls on a different date each year. It can be as early as December or as late as March, though it usually falls in January or February.

In old times, the New Year was about the only holiday the lower classes had. To this day, stores are shut for several days and businesses come to a standstill while boss and worker hold family reunions, enjoy huge feasts, gamble a little "for luck" (unless they lose!) and visit relatives and friends.

At the stroke of midnight, some parts of the large towns burst into a cacophony of fireworks. Fire crackers are supposed to drive out evil spirits. They also entertain small boys, not excluding fathers. A middle-class family is likely to spend US$40 to US$190 on fireworks.

On New Year's Day, when visitors come to each Open House, the boys are likely to fire off a volley of crackers each time a particularly respected guest makes his way up the garden path. By the second or third day supplies are mercifully exhausted.

From the second day of the Chinese New Year until the 15th day, the lions make the rounds. Acrobatic troupes bearing a pair of majestic lion heads are invited into private houses and shophouses to bless the premises. The lion, manned by two dancers, prances up and down to the sound of gongs and drums. In and out of every room, up and down the stairs, it finally comes to the family altar where it bows profoundly to the ancestor tablets. The lion gets an *ang pow*, a red packet containing money, as a reward.

CHAP GOH MEI (January/February)

Literally the Fifteenth Day after the Chinese New Year, Chap Goh Mei fulfills the function of Twelfth Night after Christmas—it is the official end of the festivities, on a full moon night.

Modern-day Chap Goh Mei is a family dinner. Many people hang out red lanterns, or switch on electric "fairy lights." Children let off the remnant of the fireworks bought for the New Year. A special dinner is cooked.

At temples, a troupe of mediums may give displays of "fire-walking." Under the protection of a deity, the participants run or walk, barefoot, up and down a ten-foot long pit of burning charcoal. One may lie down full length, unscorched, and the others walk over him.

In the old days unmarried young ladies were taken to the waterfront on Chap Goh Mei to throw oranges into the river or the sea and wish for good husbands. The young men of the town just happened to be strolling along the quays when the rickshaws came into view, dressed up to the nines, gleaming with hair oil. Flirtations had to be conducted with the utmost care as each vehicle contained at least one chaperone, a crusty old aunt who kept an eagle eye on her pretty young charge.

Traditionally, to express thanks to the gods for a good harvest, Tamil Hindus make offerings of rice on Thaiponggal. In Malaysia, while not many Tamil Hindus are farmers, this festival is still celebrated. During the celebration, at dawn, vegetarian foods are presented to the gods, and a display of fruit and flowers is assembled so that children's eyes see a vision of beauty first thing in the morning.

THAIPONGGAL (January)

Thaiponggal is a harvest festival celebrated by Tamil Hindus in Malaysia; it is fixed according to the Hindu calendar. Farmers rise while it is still dark, and cook some of the newly harvested grain to present it to the sun at dawn. This is the *ponggal*.

Some urban families have adapted this ritual to their living conditions. The family rises, bathes and gets dressed before dawn, without using any light. When all are ready in their best clothes, they assemble around a display of fruit and flowers. Lamps are lit. The first sight in the morning must be a vision of natural beauty. Dawn rises, and a vegetarian breakfast is enjoyed by all.

THAIPUSAM (January/February)

This festival is celebrated in the streets, with all the noise and excitement of a carnival.

The day is consecrated to the Hindu deity Lord Murugan, with the fulfillment of vows made to him during the year.

Devotees march in a long, colorful procession. Libations of milk and honey are made to the god and colorful displays of flowers and fruit are carried.

Those redeeming vows carry *kavadi*, fancifully decorated structures which are supported by the devotee's body; literally so—a *kavadi* may be pinned up by skewers inserted into the bearer's back and arms or attached to his flesh by steel hooks and chains; to increase the penance he may have skewers stuck through his cheeks or tongue.

The amazing part of a *kavadi* procession is not how seemingly easily the entranced penitents carry their burdens, but the fact that half an hour after the event they have neither wounds nor swellings on their bodies!

As a *kavadi* carrier marches with the procession of devotees, helpers walk quietly alongside, offering either a gentle hand or prayers. A zealous helper may whip the repenters to spur them on.

KADAZAN HARVEST FESTIVAL (May 30/31)

This is a festival observed in the East Malaysian State of Sabah. While it is named after the major indigenous tribe, the Kadazan, all Sabah natives keep the solemnity, while other Sabahans come and join in the fun.

This holiday is based on the Kadazan's worship of ancient gods, including the rice spirit Bambaazon who is revered in the rice plant, the rice grain and the cooked rice. Without rice there is no life—Kadazan children are taught from an early age that they must not spill or waste the precious grain, and that after a good harvest special respects must be paid.

Harvest festival is a time when many Sabah natives take their traditional costumes out of storage and put them on for the day. The event is celebrated with public gatherings and family parties, and Open House to all comers. *Air tapai,* the homemade rice wine, is freely available to all.

GAWAI DAYAK (June 1/2)

The Gawai Dayak has only been celebrated as a public holiday since 1964. All Sarawak's indigenous tribes have been keeping their own harvest festivals, at their own times, but the establishment of the Gawai puts it all on an official footing.

Gawai is kept in towns as well as longhouses, with traditional costume parades and competitions; for some people this is the only time in the year that they wear the beautiful but somewhat cumbersome outfits. The Iban maiden's silver jewelry is on display during the Gawai, as are the Orang Ulu's priceless antique beads.

Gawai Dayak is celebrated with an Open House, official parties and receptions, and streams of *tuak*, homemade rice wine. In longhouses, offerings of food are made to the gods of rice and prosperity, and blessed by waving a chicken over the display.

Gawai is celebrated by the *Jagoi Dayak* in Western Sarawak. The elders seated and partaking of a meal "on behalf of the ancestral spirits" are leaders of the tribal cult. The women guard the *padi* seed in covered baskets; this grain will be used to plant the fields a few months after this Gawai.

MOSLEM FESTIVALS

HARI RAYA PUASA This marks the end of the fasting month of Ramadan. Houses are cleaned and given a new coat of paint, new curtains made, new clothes sewn, and huge quantities of special foods are prepared.

In the morning of Hari Raya, the men and boys go to mosque for prayers after which families visit the graves of departed loved ones. The rest of the day is spent visiting the homes of friends and relatives where huge quantities of food is pressed on all.

HARI RAYA HAJI This festival commemorates Abraham's animal sacrifice to God in place of his son, Ismail. The men attend the Sembahyang Hari Raya Haji service at the mosque, after which animal sacrifices are performed by those who wish to do so.

For Moslems performing the *haj*, or pilgrimage, in Mecca, prayers offered on this day mark the end of the pilgrimage.

MA'AL HIJRAH The anniversary of the Prophet Mohammed's flight from Mecca to Medina, Ma'al Hijrah is the effective beginning of Islam as a separate religion. It counts as the New Year in Moslem countries.

According to this reckoning, 1989 was the year 1409H until the date of Ma'al Hijrah. The year 1410H started on August 3, which is also the first day of the month of Muharam.

PROPHET MOHAMMED'S BIRTHDAY The birthday of the founder of Islam, Prophet Mohammed, is commemorated by the Moslems. It falls on the twelfth day of the month of Rabiulawal or, in 1989, on October 12. As a public holiday, Prophet Mohammed's birthday is celebrated with special prayers, processions and religious rallies.

OTHER FESTIVALS

Other major festivals celebrated in Malaysia include Vesak Day, celebrated by the Buddhists with visits to the temples; Deepavali, an important Hindu festival celebrated among the Indian Hindus (see page 63); and Christmas, though not in as big a way as in America.

Hari Raya Haji is also known as Hari Raya Korban, the festival of sacrifice, in commemoration of the animal sacrifice Abraham offered to Allah in place of his son, Ismail, Allah's choice of sacrifice. Moslems offer animal sacrifices, usually sheep, the flesh of which is distributed to the poor.

An open-air morning market where fresh food is sold daily.

FOOD

HAVE YOU EATEN?

"HAVE YOU EATEN YOUR RICE?" is a common greeting in Malaysia. With few exceptions, everybody eats rice at least once a day. Other foods are cooked to "give flavor to the rice," which may be served in a bowl and shoveled into the mouth with chopsticks, served on a plate and eaten with fork and spoon, or served on a leaf and eaten by hand.

Fresh food is available all the year round. Vegetables are bought at the market every day by careful housewives, as are small amounts of meat, chicken or fish.

Fish is a universal favorite in Malaysia. No town, no village is far from a river or the sea. Young boys and old grannies fish with lines, with baskets or set fish traps. Many coastal farmers are part-time fishermen. Adherents of all religions can eat fish. Connoisseurs claim that meat has "a smell" from which fish is free.

Meat is cooked in soups, or the ubiquitous curry, but always cut before serving. The western style of bringing a whole roast chicken to the table for the master of the house to carve strikes Malaysians as funny. As for steaks…how would you tackle them with chopsticks?

A stall in the market selling fresh fish.

Above: **Nowadays, the Chinese use the traditional charcoal stove only for brewing herbal soups and simmering smooth** *congee*, **or porridge.**

Below: **A longhouse hearth. Fish is being cooked in the bamboo tubes (right).**

WHAT'S COOKING?

In town areas, bottled gas or electricity is used for cooking. In Miri, Sarawak, gas is piped throughout the town and sold to consumers cheaply. Microwave ovens, automatic rice cookers and toasters—all the labor-saving kitchen devices of modern times—have made their appearance in Malaysia.

In the country many housewives have gas stoves too, while some use kerosene burners. The traditional village hearth is a clay slab on the kitchen floor or on a ledge. Here a fire is kindled in the morning, and the cooking pots stood over it on iron tripods or stones. Fish is laid across green branches to grill or suspended at a height to smoke.

The old-fashioned Chinese housewife uses a charcoal stove, a round pot with a small grate in which a charcoal fire is fanned to life. Not many households today rely entirely on this fuel, but if a power cut occurs, a housewife may be glad of a charcoal pot on standby in the kitchen corner!

Strict Hindus of high caste have complicated and demanding dietary laws, one of which demands that all their food be cooked in pure brass pots. The modern alternative is stainless steel. Some families keep one set of utensils for the orthodox members and a separate one for the more liberal.

Young women of all races are advised not to sing in the kitchen. It would not affect the food, but the musical cook will be fated to marry an old man!

TABLE MANNERS

A table is not necessary for "table manners!" Many Malaysians eat on clean mats spread on the floor, and they are quite as conscious of decorum as anybody else.

An essential rule, especially among Moslems, is that only the right hand may be used for eating, washed in fresh water before the meal. It is used to scoop up rice, pick tidbits from the various cooked dishes, or roll up a morsel of *sambal belacan** in a blanched leaf. The little finger is not used for holding food, the others only up to the second digit. Soup is served in individual bowls and eaten with a spoon.

After the meal, a dish of water is passed around; small children may have to wash their whole hand but anybody with good manners need only rinse the thumb and three fingers.

Casual visitors are asked to partake of any meal the family may be having. If they are formally invited guests, they may be served separately from the family.

In conservative households the women and children eat by themselves after the men have had their fill. It is a matter of some importance for a boy to be promoted to eat with his father. This may be after he has passed important school examinations or some such rite of passage.

The "eating order" may even be extended—men eat first, women and little children who need help with eating next. School-age children and servants eat last.

Many Malaysians eat on clean mats on the floor, using their fingers in place of fork and knife.

* A condiment of strong-smelling prawn paste, ground chillies and lime juice.

113

Rice, the staff of life, has to be treated respectfully. The grain is carried from the storage jar in a little basket. Scooping it straight into the cooking pot would be an insult. Cooked rice can be served in individual plates or in one big bowl, but the cooking pot must not be brought to the table.

FOOD TABOOS

The most obvious food taboo in an officially Moslem nation is the prohibition on pork. Pork-free food and meat slaughtered according to Moslem law are certified *halal* ("not forbidden") for the benefit of Moslems.

Hindus and Sikhs are not allowed to eat beef, though they use milk products in their diet. Some Hindus avoid eggs; others consume any food that does not involve killing.

Eggs, butter, cheese are avoided by a strict Buddhist, who gets protein from soy beans and other vegetable products.

Such restrictions can give a cook headaches. It is normal to ask guests: "Do you take pork, beef?" to sort out who may be asked to sit down to dinner with whom.

An unexpected visitor at mealtime must be offered food. He will probably decline, but he must touch a little rice offered to him on a spoon. Rudely refusing rice carries its own penalty—on his way home the churl will be bitten by a snake or a scorpion.

Home-cooked fare is eaten without comment. Sniffing food is regarded as very rude by most Malaysians. Refusing food by touching the dish with the right hand is acceptable.

DRINKING

Moslems do not drink alcohol. Some other Malaysians like to brew their own. A kind of wine called toddy can be made from sugar cane juice and the sap of several palms including coconut and the *nipah*. The bud stems of the palm are slightly cut and the juice oozing out is collected in small vessels, then emptied into a jar and fermented with or without the addition of yeast.

Good toddy is a refreshing drink slightly weaker than beer.

Borneo natives make a sort of beer out of cooked glutinous rice and homemade yeast. It tastes not unlike Japanese *sake*, though the quality is seldom standard. The drink is called *tuak* or *air tapai*.

Rice beer and toddy can be distilled into high-grade alcohol called *arrack*. Unskilled processing or the addition of other substances can make this homemade beverage dangerous. Serious illness and occasional deaths as the result of *arrack*-drinking are sometimes reported.

Malaysians like company when drinking. Some communities have proper "drinking songs." Among these, the chants of Sarawak's Kayans must hold a special place. A high-ranking chief of old refused to drink unless the woman who offered him the glass had sung a proper song, and the chorus had been repeated by all present!

Murut men drink their *air tapai* neat, through reed straws, from the earthenware jars in which the brew is aged.

Convivial Malaysians of Chinese origin like to cheer each other with shouts of *"yam seng!"* (bottoms up!) to speed their guests' consumption of fine liquor or soft drinks.

An *ulam* meal. Clockwise from top left: cabbage, *kacang botol*, *buah jering*, pounded dried prawns, chilies, *ikan parang* (wolf herring), *chin char loke*, *sambal belacan*, *buah petai* and cucumber.

AN ULAM SPREAD

Sometimes adults or children may be seen picking an oily-looking creeper leaf from a hedge or an inconspicuous fern shoot from the undergrowth. "To *ulam* with our lunch!" they explain to a curious passerby.

Ulam is a way of eating raw vegetables with rice and spicy prawn-chilli paste that is popular with all Malaysians.

Green beans are suitable for *ulam*, so are jungle vegetables of many kinds, leaves, creepers, green nuts, even chunks of cabbage crisped in iced water.

Sometimes *ulam* vegetables are blanched in boiling water for a minute or so. In a dysentery-prone area where raw food often carries germs, this is a wise precaution!

BEGEDIL *(potato cutlet)*

This is not part of an *ulam* but a delicious, spiced local version of the potato cutlet, popular with the Malaysians, and easy to make.

1 large potato
½ medium-sized onion
2 tablespoons oil
½ stalk celery
½ teaspoon nutmeg
pinch of salt
1 egg, beaten

1 Boil and mash potato.
2 Finely slice onion and fry in 1 tablespoon of oil until brown and fragrant.
3 Chop celery coarsely.
4 Mix well mashed potato, onion, celery, nutmeg and salt. Divide dough-like mixture into 6 portions. Form each portion into a small ball, then flatten to ½ inch thickness.
5 Heat remainder of oil in skillet. Dip each cutlet into beaten egg before putting into pan. Fry cutlets till golden brown, remove and drain on kitchen paper.
6   Serve hot with lettuce and tomatoes.

WEDDING FEASTS

A wedding means a feast in any culture on earth. However solemn the ceremonies, when the priests and elders have had their say there is food, glorious food. In rural areas the whole village is invited; in town, guests include as many family members and friends as the budget will stand. Or more. Some Malaysians will incur heavy debts just to give their son or daughter a grand wedding party.

One important part of Malay wedding negotiations concerns the budget for the forthcoming festivity—who pays for what, and how much can we spend? In rural areas, the groom's contribution is taken to the bride's house in a merry procession of unmarried girls carrying decorated foodstuffs, and banknotes pleated into flowers as part of the presentation. As a token of their mutual caring and sharing, the bride and groom are made to "feed" each other after the wedding ceremony.

Chinese couples announce their engagement by distributing a special kind of sweet among their families and friends. It is made of finely ground peanut and spun sugar, often packed together with slabs of peanut toffee. Love is sweet! The wedding dinner itself may consist of ten or even twelve courses, each one more choice (and expensive) than the last.

The meal for a Sikh wedding is prepared by the community's elders, in the temple. The main work of catering is taken over by a team of stalwart men expert at the production of unleavened bread and huge tubs of curries.

A rural Malay wedding procession bearing decorated foodstuffs and other gifts to the house of the bride.

PICNIC FOOD

Picnic means sandwiches and an easy day for mother to some people. Malaysians take it more seriously than that!

When the party has arrived at the picnic spot, little fires are built. Rice is boiled by the more responsible members of the group, and spices are pounded for *sambal*, or condiment. It may be served on large leaves plucked from a tree and eaten by hand, but food means RICE, regardless of where you are.

Some people bring along cold cooked rice with spicy condiment packed in a large leaf. This used to be the classic fare to take on a school picnic, prepared in hundreds of leaves by a patient matron long before dawn.

Nasi lemak, or coconut rice with spicy condiment, egg, cucumber and fish, is favorite picnic fare; it is delicious hot or cold.

Busloads of students, boy scouts, sports groups, or whoever feels inclined to go for a picnic are sure to make provisions for cooking and eating rice.

A Malaysian seaside picnic may take the whole weekend. The members of the group bring along fishing tackle, hooks and lines, nets and crab traps. Seafood and fish are flipped from the line or net straight on to a rough little grill constructed out of green sticks, and roasted to perfection.

An upcountry picnic party can no longer rely on its guns for provisions. Tinned foods are carried along, in particular fish, which is called *ikan sardin*, whether it is mackerel or tuna.

Rice dumplings wrapped in bamboo leaves are offered to the gods and eaten during the Dragon Boat Festival in remembrance of Chinese poet and patriot, Qu Yuan.

Qu Yuan, who lived in the 3rd century B.C., committed suicide by jumping into the Milu River because he could not bear to see his state suffer defeat by enemies. The peasantry, on hearing the news, went on the river in boats to look for his body. When they could not find his body, they beat on drums and threw rice dumplings into the river to keep the fish away from the body.

Thus began a tradition which is kept to this day —the making of rice dumplings and dragon boat races on the 5th day of the 5th lunar month.

Stories abound about the origin of Deepavali, the Festival of Lights. But, whichever story the Hindu subscribes to, *mitha*, or sweets, are a very important part of the festival celebrations.

Sweets, revered by the Hindus as food for the gods, are offered to deities and exchanged as a symbol of happiness and an act of goodwill. On this day too, lamps are lit at the entrance of the home and *kollam*, patterns traced out in rice, are created at the entrances of the main door and the worship room.

FOOD CAN BE GOOD FOR THE SOUL

Special sweets tell the world that a Chinese couple is engaged. A triangular rice dumpling is given to friends on the day of the Dragon Boat Festival. Romantic stories waft about the plump, rich moon cakes exchanged during the Moon Festival.

The Bidayuh of Sarawak have a New Year ceremony during which a member from each household sets out with a basket full of rice cakes. He presents each family with one piece. While he is out visiting, an emissary from each family in the village also visits his house, returning the present many times over.

At the Gawai, a harvest festival celebrated by Borneo natives, visitors are not only royally feasted, but are also pressed to take basketfuls of special cakes home with them. Let nobody say the hosts are stingy!

A Malay rice cake, the *ketupat*, is boiled in a square case of coconut leaf. For festive occasions the case can be fashioned into fish or birds, designs limited only by the skill of the manufacturer. During holiday seasons there are *ketupat*-making contests in some villages, emphasizing either speed or beauty.

Indian foods for festival consumption are beautifully colored and sometimes decorated with gold leaf. On the occasion of Deepavali, the Festival of Lights, the dividing line between Food and Art is blurred: one of the most beautiful decorations consists of large, intricate designs drawn on the floor with coloured rice paste *(kollam)*.

Ketupat, a rice cake cooked in coconut leaf. Before serving, the rice cake is cut into half and each half is then further cut into smaller pieces. It is then served on a plate with the coconut leaf casing.

EATING OUT IN MALAYSIA

The climate permits and the people's gregarious habits encourage outdoor eating all the year round.

The bigger towns have food hawker centers where dozens of kitchens are set up to prepare noodle dishes, meat dishes, vegetarian dishes, sweet dishes, savory dishes, any dish imaginable while you wait.

Traveling food hawkers serve most urban neighborhoods. They offer steamed dumplings, a variety of noodle dishes cooked on portable stoves, grilled meat, ice cream and cold drinks.

A small town, a ferry point or a river jetty is sure to have at least a couple of noodle stalls, a drinks seller, maybe a "coconut man" who lops the top off the green globe and offers the fruit's sweet water for sale.

Malaysians even like going out for breakfast. In the cool of the morning they congregate around small tables outside coffee shops, under trees or shelters. Rice gruel spooned boiling hot over a raw egg is a favorite. Salted and fried tidbits are eaten with it to add relish. Long noodles, wide noodles, fat noodles and thin noodles are prepared to the customers' tastes, with soup or dry, bland or fiercely spiced.

Under the shade of leafy trees, food vendors dish out local favorites from their kitchen-on-wheels.

Breakfast "bread" is available in the form of Indian pancakes eaten with meat or lentil curry sauces. Malaysians with conservative tastes enjoy rice for breakfast too—called *nasi lemak,* it is rice cooked with coconut milk and served with fried peanuts, boiled egg, fried small fish and pickled vegetables.

FAST FOOD

Fast food is becoming popular in Malaysia. In many towns there is now a "hamburger joint," though the product is described as "beefburgers" to reassure Moslem customers that there is no pork in it! A chicken bar of the Colonel Sanders type is a common sight in an urban shopping mall. Youngsters relish the freedom of a place not frequented by aunts and mothers. Office workers who can live without rice "grab a bite" instead of going home for lunch.

McDonald's and Kentucky Fried Chicken shops are decorated and managed like their prototypes in the United States, except that the language is, of course, Malay.

Fast food does not have to be foreign, though. A canteen-style restaurant is becoming popular in Malaysia. Here each guest has a basic plate of rice, and then chooses two to four side dishes from heated display containers. There are several curries, vegetables, tidbits including small fried fish, onion rings, peanuts and the like. This is fast food in that a person does not come into the restaurant, order his meal and then wait for it to be cooked. It is cooked and ready—but it is not "junk food!"

Many rural secondary schools in Malaysia have boarding houses. Food here is cooked in large quantities and often eaten in shifts, depending on the size of the mess hall. Each student gets a mound of rice, with a few simple side dishes for flavor, protein and vitamins.

Western fast food restaurants are becoming popular among the Malaysians, while some western tourists seek refuge in familiar surroundings from the "foreign" sights and sounds of Malaysia, stopping for a burger, a coke or a thick milk shake.

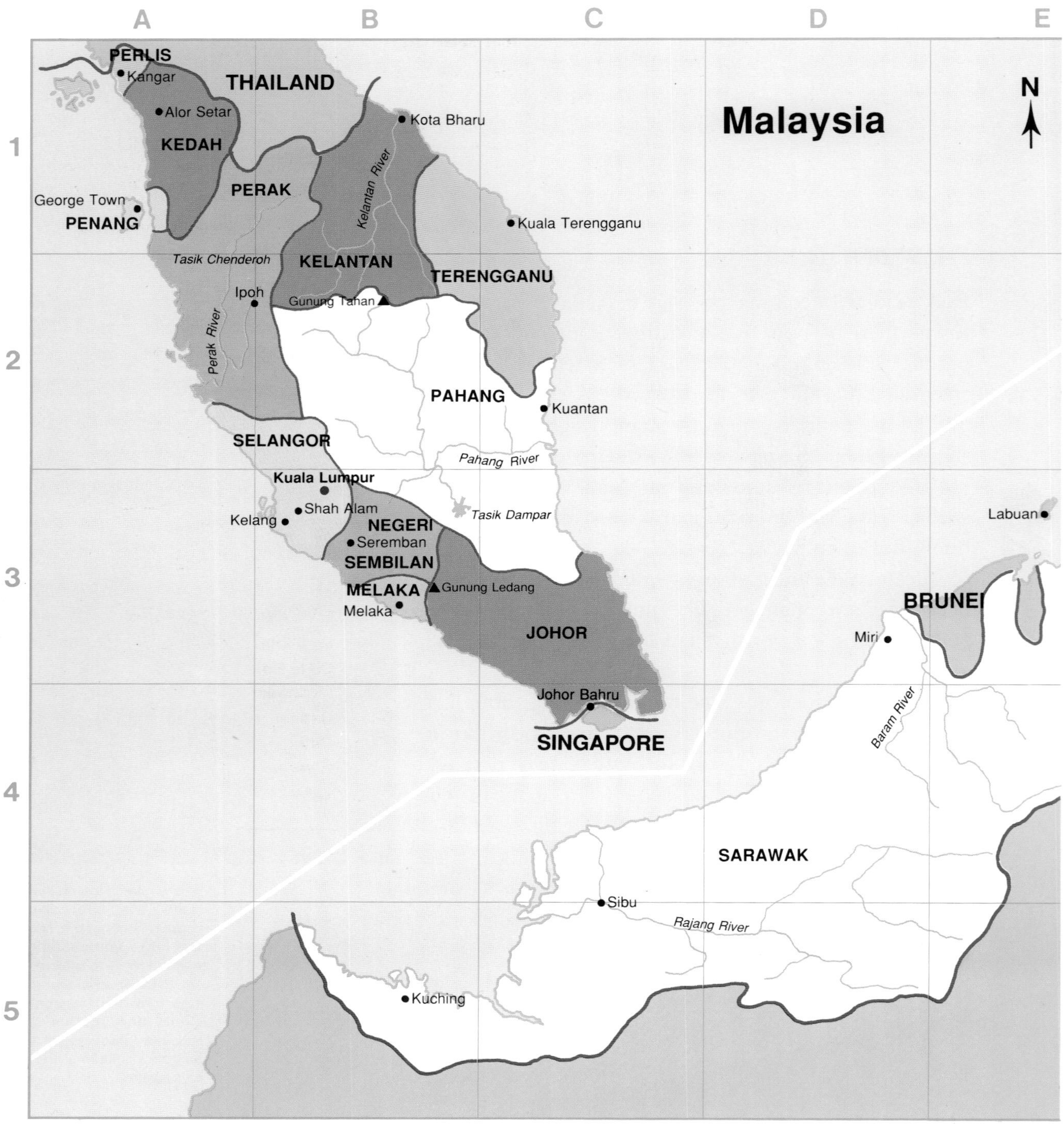

Malaysia
N
A
B
C
D
E
1
2
3
4
5
PERLIS
Kangar
THAILAND
Alor Setar
Kota Bharu
KEDAH
PERAK
Kelantan River
George Town
PENANG
Kuala Terengganu
Tasik Chenderoh
KELANTAN
TERENGGANU
Ipoh
Gunung Tahan
Perak River
PAHANG
Kuantan
SELANGOR
Pahang River
Kuala Lumpur
Shah Alam
Tasik Dampar
Kelang
NEGERI
Seremban
SEMBILAN
MELAKA
Gunung Ledang
Melaka
JOHOR
Johor Bahru
SINGAPORE
Labuan
BRUNEI
Miri
Baram River
SARAWAK
Sibu
Rajang River
Kuching

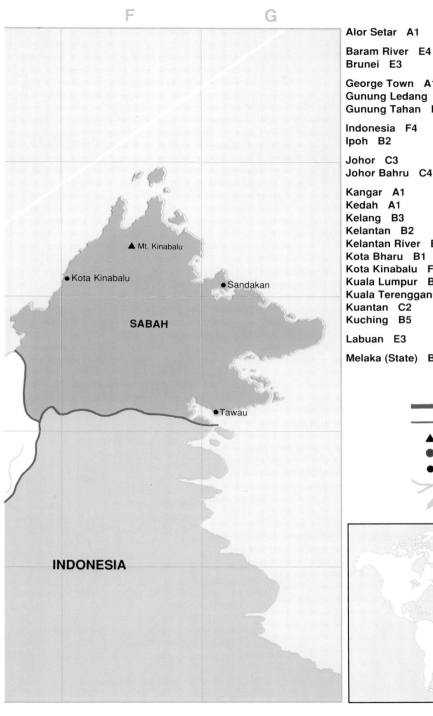

F   G

▲ Mt. Kinabalu

● Kota Kinabalu

● Sandakan

SABAH

● Tawau

INDONESIA

Alor Setar **A1**

Baram River **E4**
Brunei **E3**

George Town **A1**
Gunung Ledang **B3**
Gunung Tahan **B2**

Indonesia **F4**
Ipoh **B2**

Johor **C3**
Johor Bahru **C4**

Kangar **A1**
Kedah **A1**
Kelang **B3**
Kelantan **B2**
Kelantan River **B2**
Kota Bharu **B1**
Kota Kinabalu **F2**
Kuala Lumpur **B3**
Kuala Terengganu **C1**
Kuantan **C2**
Kuching **B5**

Labuan **E3**

Melaka (State) **B3**

Melaka **B3**
Miri **D3**
Mt. Kinabalu **F2**

Negeri Sembilan **B3**

Pahang **B2**
Pahang River **B2**
Penang **A1**
Perak **B1**
Perak River **B1**
Perlis **A1**

Rajang River **E4**

Sabah **F3**
Sandakan **G2**
Sarawak **D4**
Selangor **B2**
Seremban **B3**
Shah Alam **B3**
Sibu **C4**
Singapore **C4**

Tasik Chenderoh **A1**
Tasik Dampar **B3**
Tawau **G3**
Terengganu **C2**
Thailand **B1**

International Boundary
State Boundary
▲ Mountain
● Capital
● City
River
Lake

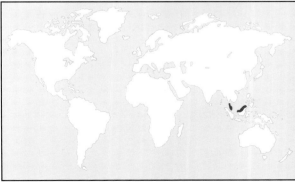

QUICK NOTES

AREA
125,565 sq miles

POPULATION
17 million

CAPITAL
Kuala Lumpur

NATIONAL FLOWER
Bunga raya (hibiscus)

NATIONAL ANTHEM
Negara Ku ("My Country")

STATES
Federal Territory, Johor, Kedah, Kelantan, Melaka, Negeri Sembilan, Pahang, Penang, Perak, Perlis, Sabah, Sarawak, Selangor and Terengganu

MAJOR RIVERS
The Kelantan, Pahang and Perak in Peninsular Malaysia, and Baram, Batang Lupar, Kinabatangan, Limbang and Rajang in East Malaysia

HIGHEST POINT
Mt. Kinabalu (13,328 feet)

OFFICIAL AND MAJOR LANGUAGES
Bahasa Malaysia (National Language) English, Mandarin and Tamil

MAJOR RELIGIONS
Islam (National Religion), Buddhism, Confucianism and Taoism, Hinduism and Christianity

CURRENCY
100 sen make one Malaysian ringgit
(US$1 = 2.7 ringgit)

MAIN EXPORTS
Electrical and electronic components, crude petroleum, natural rubber, palm oil, timber and liquefied natural gas.

IMPORTANT ANNIVERSARIES
National Day (August 31)

LEADERS IN POLITICS
Tunku Abdul Rahman—elder statesman, first Prime Minister of Malaysia
Datuk Seri Dr. Mahathir—current Prime Minister

LEADERS IN THE ARTS
Abdul Samad Said (writer)
Marion Fernandez (dancer)
Kamaluddin Muhammad (writer)
Mohd. Hoessein (artist)
Othman Awang (poet)
Yusof Ghani (artist)

GLOSSARY

gunung	mountain
kampung	village
kota	town
kuala	estuary, confluence
pantun	Malay verse
pasar	market
primary school	elementary school for children from 6 to 12 years old
pulau	island
sambal	spicy condiment of ground chillies and other spices served with rice
secondary school	high school at which children continue their schooling from 13 to 19 years old
shophouse	pre-war building in which business is carried out on the ground floor and the upper floor is used as residence by the owner's family or his workers

BIBLIOGRAPHY

Bird, I.: *The Golden Chersonese—Travels in Malaya in 1879*, Oxford University Press reprint 1980

Fauconnier, H.: *The Soul of Malaya*, English translation 1931, Oxford University Press reprint 1985

Ryan, N.J.: *The Making of Modern Malaysia and Singapore*, Oxford University Press, Kuala Lumpur 1969

Wallace, A.R.: *The Malay Achipelago*, Graham Brash reprint, Singapore 1983

INDEX

Photo Credits

APA Photo Library, Wendy Chan, Barbara Dare, Jane Duff, Foto Technik, Jill Gocher, Peter Korn, Mako Sub-aquatics, Ministry of Information Malaysia, Heidi Munan, National Archives of Malaysia, Orang Asli Museum, Radio Television Malaysia, Tourist Development Corporation of Malaysia

With special thanks to:
Foon Yew Secondary School, Johor Bahru and Majlis Ugama Islam Singapura